HARLEY-DAVIDSON

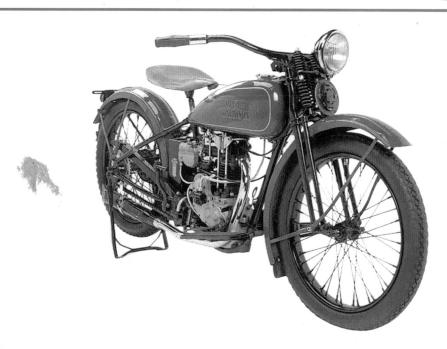

HARLEY-DAVIDSON

500 GREAT PHOTOS OF HARLEY-DAVIDSON MOTORCYCLES

Patrick Hook

This edition first published in 2003 by Crestline, an imprint of
MBI Publishing Company, Galtier Plaza, Suite 200,
380 Jackson Street, St. Paul, MN 55101-3885 USA

MBI Publishing Company books are also available at discounts
in bulk quantity for industrial or sales-promotional use.
For details write to Special Sales Manager at Motorbooks
International Wholesalers & Distributors, Galtier Plaza,
Suite 200, 380 Jackson Street, St. Paul, MN 55101-3885 USA.

ISBN 0-7603-1501-9

Designed and edited by:
FOCUS PUBLISHING, 11a St Botolph's Road, Sevenoaks,
Kent, England TN13 3AJ
Editor: Guy Croton
Designer: Neil Adams

Salamander editor: Katherine Edelston

Printed and bound in China

Contents

Introduction

A Harley-Davidson motorcycle represents different things to different people. Perhaps the most unique feature of this unmistakable machine, however, is that it is existence is an enormous paradox. While it personifies a rebel mentality, it is also a symbol of American patriotism. At the same time it is a long-established style icon, and yet an example of a cutting edge commercial product. How can all these wildly differing attributes be assigned to the same item, and especially to a motorcycle?

Well, for a start, riding a Harley makes a statement of individuality that is rivaled by few other actions. Whether the machine in question is a belt-driven veteran, a sixties chopper, or a late-model stocker, the overall message is the same—I'm riding home-grown American iron. Until recently, no other motorcycle could be visually mistaken for the real thing. The flood of clones that has appeared over the last few years—most from the Land of the Rising Sun—may look convincing from a distance, but none of them make the grade. The engineers that created these look-a-likes have tried desperately hard to incorporate the character and feel of the original, but they've failed every time.

Left: A Harley-Davidson classic—the FLH Electra-Glide of 1965. Thanks to a series of movie appearances and celebrity patronage, this motorcycle became an icon of the 1960s, and Harley-Davidson's most famous model.

A fake is a fake, and any enthusiast can tell the genuine item from a wannabe just from the exhaust noise. But the Harley-Davidson ethos is much deeper than just the sum of a few mechanical parts—it is an entire lifestyle. You don't have to take part in the camaraderie if you don't want to, but for many the sense of belonging is fundamental to the enjoyment and satisfaction of being an owner of Milwaukee's finest product. Ride up to an unknown biker bar on a hog, and you're among friends already. Break down at the side of the road miles from home, and before long, another Harley rider will come to your rescue. The rules of membership of this club are unwritten, but they are clear and well understood by those within it. There's a famous saying in Harley circles, that "If you have to ask, you wouldn't understand." Ultimately, the only way to find out, is to live the life, and ride the machine!

Right: Detail of a 1993 Heritage Softail Classic. This motorcycle was designed to provide a balanced package of old and new, and it succeeded admirably in this aim.

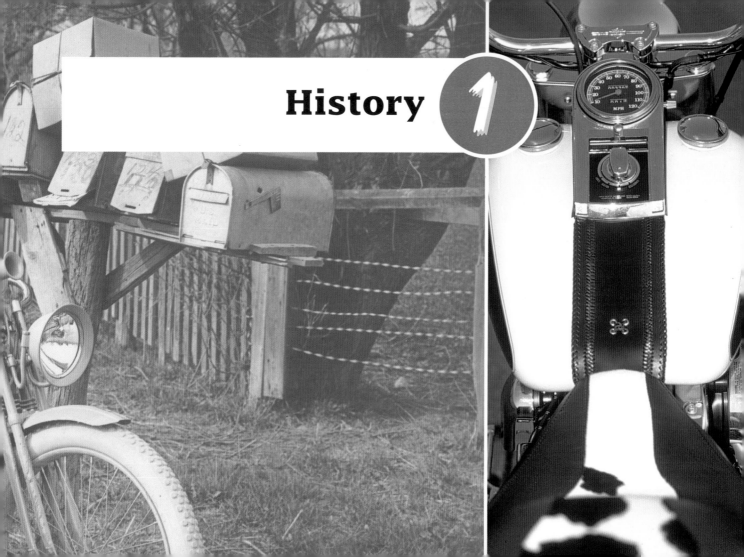

History **1**

The history of the Harley-Davidson Motor Company is a fascinating tale which begins with the vision and determination of a small group of dedicated engineers, and continues through a period of a hundred years of turmoil—both industrial and political—to the present day, when Harley-Davidson has become a huge commercial empire.

The beginnings are well known to most Harley aficionados—it all began in a small wooden shed in 1903, with a single cylinder motor bolted into what was little more than a strengthened bicycle frame. Most of the company's history is reasonably well documented, but this alone does not tell the real story of the Harley-Davidson motorcycle, for it is a machine of the people who rode it, and they represent the real history of this legendary name.

During the company's lifetime, many global events have occurred which have had significant effects on the machines which came off the production line. Three stand out, though—The Great War, the Depression, and the Second World War. While they had very different influences on Harley-Davidson production, they all helped shape it into what it is today. Other major

Above: This is where it all began! A humble wooden shed is all the fledgling company could afford in the early days—from this arose the mighty Harley-Davidson factory.

landmarks include commercial ones—the post-war era of foreign imports, the company's take-over by AMF, and the "liberation" of the company back into the hands of the management, are just a few examples.

If you were to ask a typical Harley rider about the history of the marque though, the response would be

Above: Like most of the other pioneering motorcycle factories, Harley-Davidson also made bicycles—this is a beautifully restored example of an early model.

Above: Having moved on from the original wooden shed, the founding members of the Harley-Davidson company pose for a publicity photograph.

Above: While the earliest Harley-Davidson motorcycles were superior to most of their rivals, they were still basic machines that were little more than powered bicycles.

Right: The single-cylinder engines transferred drive to the back wheel via a pulley-driven belt, as can be seen here.

likely to be more about the various machines than political or commercial events. To most contemporary riders, the model history can be divided into several categories—the Big Twins, the Sportsters, the old stuff, the racers, and the others. The Big Twins would be considered to have started out with the Knucklehead, then developed through the Panhead, the Shovelhead, up to the two generations of Evolution Blockheads. Sportsters were born out of the ill-fated Model K, from which the first XLs were created. These initially developed into hot-rods, but then tamed down considerably for many years, before also being updated to Evolution specification.

The bikes comprising the "old stuff" are generally not well known to most modern Harley riders, although most could probably name more than riders of any other make could manage for their own marque of choice. The racers would include the early board track machines, ridden by old timers from the days when men were men—tough nuts, they rode unstable bikes at high speeds with no protective clothing and little regard to safety. Many died or were horrifically injured during this

Above: While the early Harley-Davidson V-twins may look archaic today, these machines were cutting-edge technology when they were first produced.

time. Dirt track competition then got popular, and became the mainstay of American motorcycle sport, although road racing also had its adherents. While racing has got steadily safer over the years, the riders still push to the limits, and still regularly pay dearly for the love of their sport.

The "others" would be considered to include unique machines like the Servi Car—Harley-Davidson's little utility three wheeler—as well as the flood of imports that came in as a result of the company's acquisition of the Italian motorcycle factory formerly known as Aermacchi.

Although the name Harley-Davidson is synonymous with large capacity V-twins, it didn't start out that way—at the end of the nineteenth century the internal combustion engine was gradually finding its way into various forms of transportation. While most of these early vehicles had four wheels, many had two or even three. Engineers are always looking for new technologies to

Left: The founders of the Harley-Davidson company were so successful because they understood the value of marketing their product, as in this early publicity shot.

Right: Many potential Harley customers lived in remote areas, and so it was vital to display the rugged nature of the Harley-Davidson product.

play with, and before long all over the world backyard wrenches were trying to build their own interpretations of how powered transportation could best be achieved. This rush of enthusiasts included William Harley and Arthur Davidson, who built their first single cylinder motorcycle in Milwaukee in 1901. Undeterred by this machine's failings, they went on to form the Harley-Davidson company in 1903, and together with two more members of the Davidson family, started producing motorcycles.

The early Harley-Davidson machines were basic; they had a single cylinder motor with an atmospheric-inlet-valve, and developed about three horsepower—this had a $3\frac{1}{8}$ inch bore and $3\frac{1}{2}$ inch stroke, and was housed in a rudimentary chassis which bore many similarities to contemporary bicycle designs; it had belt drive, and displaced 25 ci. These were built in a wooden shed which measured 10 x 15 feet, and rather ambitiously had "Harley-Davidson Motor Company" written on the door.

Competitions were popular at the time—for the first few years these were more about endurance and the ability to get up steep hills than outright speed, since that was what mattered in the real world, on the actual roads that customers would be using. Racing success came early for these intrepid engineers—in 1905, a Harley-Davidson won a 15 mile race in Chicago, and the accompanying acclaim encouraged other customers to come forward. The resulting increase in demand enabled a move to larger premises in 1906, when a building measuring 28 x 80 feet was acquired—at the same time the first sales catalogue was produced and the workforce went up to six full-time employees.

By 1907, the fledgling factory had a good enough reputation to convince several police forces to place orders for motorcycles—this was a major step forward, both in terms of direct sales, and in terms of the very evident endorsement of the Harley-Davidson product. In 1908 there was a further boon to the company's marketing profile when Walter Davidson managed to set an economy record by recording 188.234 mpg. This, coupled with a reputation for excellent reliability, meant that sales boomed.

Above: The Harley-Davidson factory had stiff competition from other rival companies—in particular from Indian, who made first class machines.

Above: The Indian was essentially very similar to the Harley-Davidson—it had to be, because it had to meet the same demands on the same roads.

Right: It was common practice to leave the valvegear exposed, as can be seen here on the engine of this Indian V-twin.

The results of races, reliability trials, and economy runs were well publicized, and much was made about successes by the manufacturers of the winning machines. This was partly because at the time there were no laws about the veracity of advertisers claims for their products—consequently, potential purchasers never knew what they should or shouldn't believe. Open competitions were one way to sort out which manufacturers could live up to their boasts, and which couldn't.

The Harley-Davidson company scored its first major endurance race win in 1908, when Walter Davidson won the Catskill to New York race. The resulting publicity helped them enormously in the marketplace—annual production went up from 450 machines a year in 1908 to 1,149 in 1909, a staggering increase for such a small company.

In 1909, the company introduced its first V-twin—this was a fairly basic machine powered by an engine which displaced 49.5 ci. and produced 7 bhp. Many other

Left: This rig was used for training purposes, hence the cutaway areas which helped fledgling mechanics to understand the inner workings of the internal combustion engine.

manufacturers had already produced V-twins, and the Harley-Davidson factory wasted little time in following suit. The reasons for this were simple—if you were already manufacturing a single cylinder engine, basically all that was necessary to make a V-twin was to construct a different set of crankcases and a longer crankpin. Then two sets of pistons, cylinders, and heads could be bolted onto a common bottom end, creating a low-cost V-twin.

This configuration doubled the torque and power output for very little extra cost, and also fitted into the existing single cylinder chassis with very few modifications. As a result, it clearly made commercial sense to offer such machines for sale, and their much improved performance proved very popular with customers.

By 1912, the demand for Harley-Davidson machines meant that the factory was expanding at an enormous

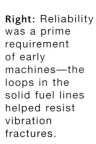

Right: Reliability was a prime requirement of early machines—the loops in the solid fuel lines helped resist vibration fractures.

Left: Sidecars proved to be very popular for distribution purposes, as exemplified by this mailman delivering bulky packages.

rate. This not only required increased production capacity, but also extra organizational facilities, and so they started constructing a new six story administration building to house the new company headquarters. This was followed in 1913 by the creation of a dedicated racing department—this allowed them to enter competition with a factory team in 1914, with William S.

Harley in charge of race engineering development. The team's excellent organization and commitment meant that they quickly dominated the sport, and soon earned the nickname the "Wrecking Crew."

During the First World War, the factory stopped racing and focussed instead on producing large numbers of machines for the military, with a total production run of 20,000 machines. This helped the company in many ways—much was learnt about optimizing production techniques, and the income generated helped stabilize finances over the tough years to come. After the war racing resumed, and many competition successes came their way as a result of a heavy investment program in research and development.

Although the nickname "Hog" has now been applied to Harleys for many years, few people actually know where it came from—it actually derives from a highly successful racing team which used a small pig as a mascot. Every time they won a race on their Harley-Davidsons, they would carry the pig on a victory lap!

At this time not all Harley-Davidson twins had "V" configurations—the 37 ci. Sport, for instance, had a horizontally-opposed flat twin engine. This model was exported in large numbers, although the domestic market was less keen on a machine which did not have

Right: As the technology was developed to generate more horsepower, so the amount of finning had to be increased to keep the engines from overheating.

a V-twin motor. Such customer resistance to new ideas would prove to be a thorn in the factory's side for many years to come.

The start of the 1920's was a period of great economic uncertainty in the United States, and worse was to come. At this time, the Harley-Davidson company was the biggest motorcycle manufacturer in the world, and luckily for them, although domestic sales had collapsed, the export market was still strong.

In 1921 the factory decided that it could not afford to stay in professional racing, and pulled out of active competition. It still won acclaim on the track though— private riders with varying amounts of factory support still achieved success. In February 1921, for instance, a Harley-Davidson entered the record books as the first motorcycle to ever win a race at an average speed of over 100 mph. This was on a board track at Fresno, California.

Although the economic depression had not really started to take effect in the early 1920's, the signs were there for all to see, and it was clear that hard times were to come. On the plus side, in 1921 they introduced their first 74 cu in. V-Twin engine, but all the same, over the next few years marketing focussed on economy, reduced prices, and the suitability of Harley-Davidson's for sidecar work, rather than on outright performance.

Left: The span of the handlebars on early machines seems strange in the modern world, but back then the roads were so bad that maximum control was vital.

In 1928 the model JD was released. For its time, the twin-cam powered machine was an incredible performer—it could achieve speeds of up to 100 mph, when most other motorcycles would struggle to maintain anything more than 60 mph. Not all machines produced at this time had an emphasis on performance, though—the incredibly successful flathead 45 ci. engine was introduced in 1929. Initially released in the D model, it was intended to power a wide range of utility models, and went on to be manufactured for longer than any other motorcycle in history.

By this stage, production was back up to more than 20,000, and just as it looked as though the economy might have fully recovered, in 1929 the New York stock market crashed heavily. Of the three hundred or so manufacturers who produced motorcycles before the First World War, due to the economic uncertainty and tough marketplace of the period leading up to the early 1930s, only Indian and Harley-Davidson remained.

During the Great Depression, the factory had to economize by making many cutbacks, and one of the greatest overheads it had to cope with was the payroll;

Above: Although the Harley-Davidson name became synonymous with V-twins, for many years single-cylinder machines were an important part of the model range.

Left: As engine designs were refined over the years, the valvegear became enclosed, allowing service intervals to be extended, and oil consumption to be reduced.

Opposite: It is ironic that horse-drawn trailers were used to deliver motorcycles, although the railroads would have been used for anything more than small distances.

in order to avoid redundancies, job schedules were rearranged so that many employees only worked two days a week. This brought great hardship to their families, but matters would have been worse had the factory closed. The management were far from complacent about the weak marketplace—they tried lots of different methods to liven up the model range in an attempt to increase sales. This included improving the visual appeal of the bikes by offering more exciting combinations of colors, and enhancing paint schemes by using art-deco graphics—such as the eagle design which was painted onto gas tanks of all bikes in the model range, with the exception of special orders.

The drive to create sales meant that all possible corners of the market had to be considered. As a result, many unlikely concepts were assessed, one of which became reality as a general purpose utility vehicle, and thus the Servi-Car was born. Powered by the flathead 45 ci. engine, it was introduced in 1932, and went on to become the longest running model in the Harley-Davidson factory's history.

Even though the company was doing its best to generate further sales, in 1933 they fell to the lowest figures for any year since 1910, with a total run of only

3,700 machines. It is a credit to the company that they managed to stay afloat during these hard times. Somehow they managed to not only struggle through, but also to develop new models. These included the first of the now infamous "Big Twins," which was introduced in 1936 in the form of the EL, which most people would go on to refer to as the Knucklehead. This had an overhead valve 61 ci. motor which was a massive step forward—once the initial teething problems had been sorted out. The year 1936 also saw the introduction of the 80 ci. flathead. This was a low performance machine which was intended for utilitarian use, such as hauling sidecars. Matters were improving by this stage, with a total of 9,812 bikes being produced by the factory.

The years leading up to the Second World War saw a resurgence in sales, and the factory made what they could of competition successes, such as in 1937 when a 61 ci. Harley-Davidson powered machine set a new motorcycle land speed record. It was ridden by a famous racer called Joe Petrali, who ran through the traps at 136.183 mph.

Left: The Knucklehead was so-called because of the two large nuts on the cylinder heads—to some they looked like a clenched fist.

The introduction of new models continued in 1937, with the release of the first of the WL range. The WL formed the basis of what became an enormous production run of military machines during World War Two; from just after the attack on Pearl Harbor until peace was declared, the factory devoted its entire production to military machines, and some 90,000 WLAs were manufactured in total. Although WL based machines dominated production, other military machines were also manufactured, including the XA model. This used a horizontally-opposed flat-twin engine with shaft drive to the rear wheel. It was intended for use in the deserts of North Africa, where vast areas of sandy terrain had proved a problem to machines with conventional top-heavy chain-driven layouts. The success of the allied campaign against the forces of Rommel's Africa Korps in North Africa was a huge step forward in the struggle with Nazism. It was, however, unfortunate for the factory, as the XA's specific attributes were no longer required. This meant that its heavy investments in development time and effort were wasted, and only about 1,000 XAs were ever built.

During the war, many thousands of American servicemen all over the world became familiar with everyday life with the Harley-Davidson. This close association with the marque was to have great significance when the war ended and these men came home, for a large number of them sought out and purchased their very own American-made motorcycles for private use.

Above: The 45 made a superb workhorse for military use, and the great numbers produced by the factory helped them survive the loss of civilian sales during the war.

When hostilities finally ended with the eventual surrender of both the Nazi and Japanese forces, the Allies seized many German industrial assets in reparations. These included the manufacturing rights to the DKW two-stroke, and the Harley-Davidson factory wasted little time in releasing a machine directly copied from these designs when they introduced the 125S. This went on to become the Hummer, and larger versions were produced later in capacities of 165 and 175 cc.

Although the vast network of Harley-Davidson dealers were generally disinterested in promoting the sales of small two-strokes, these machines proved very popular as learner bikes for young people. This introduced vast numbers of novice riders to the Harley-Davidson marque, and created a brand loyalty that paid immense dividends as these customers grew older and purchased larger machines. It took the factory some time to realize that this was a great long-term way to generate sales, but once they did, they did much to ensure that novice riders would always have an entry-level Harley-Davidson available to them.

Left: When the war ended, great efforts were made to stimulate sales by using bright colors and many polished chrome parts.

Right: As can be seen here, almost everything except the frame was painted or chromed —it must have been hard work keeping such a machine good and clean!

Once peace had returned to the western world, the factory once again got involved with racing. Technical lessons learned during the war were used to improve machines right across the model range. Such improvements included enhancements to production techniques, better metallurgy for component manufacture, advancements in machine tool design, and so on. There were shortages of certain materials, however—these included a lack of chromium and nickel, which meant that the use of stainless

Right: As the performance of motorcycles improved, so riders also needed to see where they were going, hence the fitment of large headlights.

Right: The marketing department went to great lengths to portray life with a Harley-Davidson as being good, clean, wholesome fun!

steel and chrome plate had to be limited. The mineral ores for these and other materials often had to come from overseas, and pre-war stockpiles had all been used up by the massive amount of high-priority military equipment manufactured during this period.

The WR racer was introduced in 1946; this used a specially built 45 ci. flathead racing engine derived from the road model—it went on to achieve great success in all manner of competitions for more than two decades.

Although the Knucklehead engine had proved very popular with customers, it was getting a bit long in the

Enjoy Motorcycling More

with

HARLEY-DAVIDSON ACCESSORIES

Everything for the Motorcyclist
APPROVED MOTORCYCLE ACCESSORIES
for 1940

IF YOUR DEALER CANNOT SUPPLY YOU ... WRITE DIRECT TO
HARLEY - DAVIDSON MOTOR CO.
MILWAUKEE, WISCONSIN, U.S.A.
IN U.S. DOLLARS F. O. B. MILWAUKEE, WIS., U.S.A. ALL DUTIES, TAXES, TRANSPORTATION, EXTRA.
QUOTED SUBJECT TO CHANGE WITHOUT NOTICE

Above: The Indian factory was in real financial trouble after the war, and they did their best to survive by producing beautifully styled machines.

Above: The Indian emblem was distinctive, and even though many customers were loyal to the end, it was not enough to save the marque from ruin.

tooth, and was replaced in 1948 by the Panhead. This powerplant was available in 61 and 74 ci., and had hydraulic lifters and aluminum cylinder heads. The economic climate in the post-war years allowed the factory to recover from the desperate situation of the 1930s—in ten years they had managed to increase production from under 10,000 machines a year to over 30,000—and total factory production in 1948 was 31,163 machines.

The factory continued to introduce new features to the model range throughout the late 1940s, including, in 1949, the fitment of hydraulic front forks to a model powered by the new Panhead engine called the Hydra-Glide. This provided a marked improvement in the ride quality, although as the machine had no rear suspension, it still relied heavily on the isolation abilities of the sprung seat.

The early 1950s saw the introduction of the K model. Although this motorcycle was a disappointment in terms of sales, it proved to be the foundation stone of a highly successful lineage of sports machines. The racing brother of the K model was the KR—although

Above: A view from the rider's perspective shows how elaborate the detailing was—the problem was, these machines were just too expensive to manufacture.

the engines looked more or less identical, they were in fact very different animals. The KR was a highly competitive machine, and in 1953 it won the big race at Daytona. This was highly significant for Harley-Davidson, since a Norton had won it for the previous three years running.

The year 1953 was one of make or break for American motorcycle manufacturers. While Harley-Davidson was celebrating its 50th Anniversary, rival company Indian went out of business, leaving Milwaukee to represent the United States in the world market.

Above: When the Panhead engine was released, it continued the tradition of being named after the shape of its rocker covers.

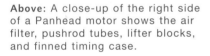

Above: A close-up of the right side of a Panhead motor shows the air filter, pushrod tubes, lifter blocks, and finned timing case.

Right: In order to keep the exhausts looking shiny, they were hidden behind spiral coverings—this stopped the heat from bluing the chrome.

The K model only survived in its original form until 1953, when various attempts were made to improve its dismal performance. In 1957, however, the factory excelled itself by introducing a new variant of the K engine with overhead valves—this was the first Sportster, which was designated the "XL." This Harley-Davidson proved a tremendous hit in the marketplace, and once the factory released a high performance model called the XLCH, they struggled to keep up with demand.

The factory finally caught up with the rest of the world in 1958, when they at last brought hydraulic rear suspension to the Big Twin range with the introduction of the Duo Glide.

Whilst the 1950s ended on a high with the success of the plush Panhead-engined big twins and the hot-rod performance of the XLCH, the 1960s were to prove very different for the fortunes of the Harley-Davidson company. Omens looked good initially—the economy was healthy, and sales of motorcycles were booming. Although few noticed at the time, Honda made a quiet entry into the marketplace with a small economy machine, setting the scene for many tens of thousands of other Japanese motorcycles to flood into the United States over the next few years.

Harley-Davidson's answer to the influx of foreign utility machines was to release the Topper scooter. This poorly thought-out model was an unmitigated sales disaster, and the

Right: This customized Panhead is the epitome of style to many, with its fishtail pipes, high bars, and kicked-out front end.

factory never tried to enter the scooter market again. One of the biggest problems the company had to deal with when trying to compete in the utility market was that such machines sold on the basis of cost—American labor was expensive, and the two factors had to be resolved somehow. The management decided to source machines from abroad and re-label them as Harley-

Davidsons—what is referred to these days as "badge engineering." The company's solution was to purchase a half share in the ailing Italian firm of Aermacchi, and import their range of small machines for sale at prices that would be much more realistic than could be achieved with home-built examples.

By the mid 1960s it had become clear to the management that a massive reinvestment in machine tooling was going to be required if the factory was to remain competitive—in 1965 they finally decided to go public to finance the necessary production equipment. One of the company's most

famous models of all time was introduced in the same year; it was effectively an electric-start version of the Duo Glide, and was the immensely successful Electra Glide. The machine captured the spirit of the times, and became an icon of the period, appearing in many famous movies, including *Electra Glide in Blue* and the all-time classic, *Easy Rider*.

The following year, 1966, saw the replacement of the under-powered Panhead engine with an updated powerplant which used new cylinder heads based on those from the Sportster. This new engine was quickly nicknamed the "Shovelhead," and it soon proved a hit with the customers, and quickly acquired a loyal following. Although the Big Twin and Sportster range was continually being updated, they were left lagging behind by the new street machines imported from Europe and Japan. This foreign dominance did not

Left: The image of the Harley-Davidson was heavily influenced by competition results. This WR was one of the most successful racers the factory ever produced.

Above: The introduction of small Italian imports was a big shock to the traditionalists, but it was in a genuine attempt to compete with the Japanese on their own terms.

Right: Wherever you go in the world, Harley-Davidson enthusiasts will gather together for meets, rallies, runs, and just plain old good times!

carry over to the race-track, though—in 1969 the legendary rider Cal Rayborn took a KR to back to back races at the Daytona 200.

The Harley-Davidson factory did not only face threats at the track, though; in 1969 they had to face up to the possibility of a hostile take-over by a company called Bango-Punta, and so they moved quickly to merge with a sports-products conglomerate known as AMF, which

stood for American Machine and Foundry. This association allowed the company to invest further, and a new manufacturing plant was built at York, Pennsylvania.

This influx of investment money did not come without strings, however, and the new AMF board members demanded that the price of bikes was raised to pay for it. The board also pushed for far higher sales

Far left: The alternator-Shovel engine is distinguished by the shape of the timing cover. First produced as a 74, this one is an 80 cube.

Left: Factory air cleaner covers are generally one of the first things customers replace after collecting a new machine, as can be seen here.

volumes, and the ensuing production shortcuts lowered the quality of the bikes they manufactured. This was the start of a very difficult time, both for the factory and for the unfortunate customers who had to suffer the consequences—it was not long before decline set in.

Although the union with AMF was not always a happy one, it is doubtful if Harley-Davidson could have survived the 1970s without them. The chairman of AMF was a man called Rodney Gott—he had been a Harley fan since before the Second World War, and so was not the "evil businessman" that many in the press portrayed him as.

In 1970, Cal Rayborn once again hit the headlines by breaking the motorcycle world land speed record on the Bonneville salt flats, at just over 265 mph. The machine looked more like a giant cigar than a bike—it was sixteen

Above: Electra-Glide—the most famous name in motorcycling! This machine set a trend that helped define the 1960s, eventually becoming a style icon.

Above right: Check out fifty Electra-Glides, and every one of them will be different—from paintwork to chrome, seats to handlebars, and pipes to fenders.

Right: This machine retains the original exhaust pipes and mufflers, but the paintwork and chrome have been much improved from stock.

Above: This sign says it all. Juneau Avenue is the very heart of the Harley-Davidson company, and is a mecca to many tens of thousands of loyal fans.

feet long, with streamlined bodywork, and powered by a highly tuned Sportster engine. The following year, 1971, the Super Glide appeared; this was a seminal machine—it was the first true factory custom bike, and set the trend for Harley-Davidson models right up to the present day.

In 1971 the nine-second barrier was broken in motorcycle drag racing by a Harley-Davidson powered machine ridden by Joe Smith. It is somewhat ironic that sports bike fans often mock Harley-Davidsons for being slow, and yet for years they dominated the sports of dirt track and drag racing, and, in many classes, still do.

In the early 1970s the company continued to expand its facilities, and in 1973 all the factory's assembly operations were moved to a modern 400,000 square foot plant in York, Penn., although all other production operations remained in Milwaukee and Tomahawk. This increased production capability played a significant part in raising total sales to 75,403 motorcycles in 1975.

Competition successes were still coming in thick and fast in the mid 1970s—Harley-Davidson won the AMA Grand National Championships in dirt track racing for four years in a row, starting in 1975 with a machine ridden by Gary Scott, then between 1976 and 1978 the great Jay Springsteen took the honors.

The creation of the "factory custom" back in 1971 with the release of the Super Glide had inspired many other manufacturers to create their own interpretations of the theme, but few achieved notable success. In 1977, the Harley-Davidson factory moved the goal posts once again by introducing the public to the FXS "Low Rider." This had drag handlebars, a low seating position, and other special styling parts. It was very well-received by the buying public, something that cannot be said for the other new machine released the same year, the XLCR Café Racer. This was an upmarket Sportster, which was beautifully styled in the manner of flat trackers; it failed to catch on, however. This was mainly because the market it was aimed at—sports enthusiasts—could buy all the performance they wanted at far lower prices by purchasing any one of a number of contemporary Japanese superbikes.

The Harley-Davidson factory had tired of trying to convince the market to buy under-powered and over-priced import machines, and in 1978 they finally sold off the old Aermacchi concern. By this stage the factory's proportion of big-bike sales had fallen from 80% in the 1960s to a miserable figure of less than 20% in 1979.

The 1980s would prove to be a decade of great change for the Harley-Davidson company. Things started out quietly with the release of a new touring model with a rubber mounted Shovelhead engine and a bolted-on transmission. Although this machine was not really a ground breaker, it was a significant step forward, and it managed to achieve critical acclaim in the press, who gave it the title "King of the Highway."

Above: The modern air-conditioned hi-tech buildings show that the company has come a long way from its humble wooden shed origins.

Above: The loyalty of the Harley-Davidson staff to their product is almost unique in the modern manufacturing world.

Above: Why be humble? As they say, "If you've got it, flaunt it!" This sign points the way to Harley-Davidson company headquarters.

It was not until 1981 that big changes happened. An amicable divorce from AMF was signaled when thirteen senior Harley-Davidson executives signed a letter of intent to purchase the Harley-Davidson Motor Company; the move was funded by investment financiers Citicorp. The change of power within the company had immediate consequences at all levels—the new management had been planning many changes, and one of the first was the implementation in 1982 of the Materials as Needed (MAN) program. This was a system whereby the stocks of raw materials and externally-sourced components held by the company were reduced to an absolute minimum. This saved on storage costs, but also meant that interest was no longer being paid on bank loans to finance parts that would sit on a shelf for months before being used. It required skilled management to ensure that the principle would work though, for a whole production line could be halted if just one vital part was out of stock.

Left: When Willie G. Davidson decided to pay homage to the success of the XR750, he designed the XR1000. This was surely one of the most beautiful machines ever to leave the Harley-Davidson factory.

The new management team also capitalized on the brand loyalty of their customers by forming the Harley Owners Group (H.O.G.) in 1983. This went on to become the largest of its kind in the world, and allowed the company to maintain contact with its customers, as well as to foster the relationship through special product offers, meetings, newsletters, and all manner of other

Above right: This way to Harley heaven! Juneau Avenue was the site of factory Number Two.

Right: Although this building is home to one of the main factory production facilities, these days it is just one of many—a far cry from the early days.

Above: The release of the Evolution engine was a revolution. Soon nicknamed the Blockhead, it was a major design improvement over the Shovelhead.

benefits. In many ways, this has become the role model for almost all the other automotive companies in the world, most of whom couldn't even dream of achieving 10% of the brand following that Harley-Davidson enjoys.

Harley-Davidson also went on the offensive in 1983, by claiming that the Japanese motorcycle manufacturers were creating huge stockpiles of unsold machines on American soil, and that this constituted unfair trading practice. After much petitioning, the International Trade Commission (ITC) agreed, and a tariff was imposed on all imported Japanese motorcycles which had engines of 700cc or more. This import tax was to last for five years, during which time the company argued that they would be able to build up both their resources and their market share, so that they would be able to compete on more even terms.

In 1984 the factory finally showed the results of its intensive seven year development program when they released the first Evolution-powered machines. This engine was, as its name implied, a direct evolution from the old Shovelhead. It featured revisions to almost every single component, and was an enormous step forward.

The engine no longer leaked oil, was more reliable, produced lower exhaust emissions, and was more powerful than its predecessor. Five new models were introduced, including the famous Softail, with its revolutionary new rear suspension system, featuring shock absorbers hidden under the transmission.

The success of the Evolution-engined models was clear for all to see, and in 1986 the management felt that the prognosis for the company was good enough to return to public ownership, and preparations duly began. The Evolution-engined Sportster was also introduced in 1986 —initially this was only available in 883 cc form, but it was followed shortly by an 1100 cc version.

In 1987, the Harley-Davidson company was approved for listing on the New York Stock Exchange. This raised further capital, much of which was plowed straight back

Above: The design of the twin-cam version of the Evolution engine provided for improved pushrod geometry, reducing engine noise and allowing higher rpm.

Right: The rider's view on this late model machine hasn't changed much since the 1950s—a feature that suits most owners just fine.

into research and development for future models. In the same year the factory started a new scheme called the "Buy Back Program"—this was designed to encourage new customers to purchase a Harley-Davidson, and then trade it in at full value within two years. Ultimately,

Above: The use of a 21 inch front wheel and high handlebars gives a chopper look to this bike without the need for fitting longer forks.

it was really intended to allow someone who was new to the marque to start out on a Sportster, ride it for a while, and then, when they were ready, to trade it back against a Big Twin. Consequently, the program only applied to certain models.

Since tradition has always been one of the mainstays of the Harley-Davidson ethos, the retro look was a natural choice for the styling department, and they took full advantage of this when they released the FXSTS Springer Softail in 1988. This model featured a springer front end, just like the bikes of old, and it sold well. A 1200 cc version of the Evolution-engined Sportster was also released in 1988, and this proved to be a great success in the marketplace.

The 1990s started out with the introduction of the FLSTF Fat Boy—a machine which introduced a whole new look to the model range. It became an overnight success, and went on to spawn many variants. The Fat Boy was followed up in 1991 by the Dyna Glide, and the five speed transmission became standard right across the model range. Drive trains were further standardized in 1992 when belt drive became a universal fitment.

The same year, Harley-Davidson broadened its portfolio by purchasing a minority share in the Buell Motorcycle Company. This was a facility which made sports bikes using the XL883 Sportster engine.

When the factory celebrated its 90th Anniversary in 1993, somewhere in the region of 100,000 riders congregated in Milwaukee for a massive "Family Reunion" parade. This was an incredible eight miles long, and featured about 60,000 Harley-Davidsons.

The factory's long association with motorcycle competition led to aspirations of achieving success in Superbike racing; the plan was to take part in the domestic championship, and when this was in the bag, to go on and win the World Championship title. Sadly, misguided patriotism took the place of sense, and the decision was made to use only American-made components. This compromised the machine they built before it ever reached the track. No suitable racing parts were made in the United States at the time, and trying to compete at this level and develop an entire motorcycle was beyond the capabilities of a small racing department—not even Honda would have taken on such a challenge. The resulting bike—the VR1000—was

Right: A completely stock Harley-Davidson is a rare sight! Wrinkle finish black paint and polished fins provide excellent detailing on this Evolution engine.

a good machine, but even when piloted by ex-Grand Prix riders was incapable of winning. It lived on for a couple of seasons, but then sank into obscurity.

By the mid-1990s, development was well under way on the new generation of Evolution engines, and so interim machines were really only stop-gap models. In 1995 sales figures passed the 100,000 mark, and the first fuel-injected engines were introduced. The Heritage Springer Softail was released in 1996, and the new 88 ci. twin cam engines were finally announced in 1998, although they didn't hit the marketplace until 1999. Bristling with updated features, the new machines lived up to the promises made by the marketing department, and sales were excellent.

The new millennium saw the Softail receive an even newer version of the twin cam, which had a vibration suppresser incorporated to make the ride smoother. Later in the year, all Softail models were produced with fuel injection, to reduce emissions and improve fuel economy.

Left: The retro look is very popular on modern machines, with styling cues straight from the '50s.

Right: The solid wheels and wide tires give the Fat Boy a distinctive and popular look.

Right: Rising like a phoenix from the ashes, the formation of a new Indian company has already produced spectacular machines.

In 2002 the V-Rod was released to an awe-struck public. This motorcycle was the first entirely new design to have come out of the factory in decades. The 60 degree engine was derived from the VR1000 Superbike, but rubber mounted and equipped with a balancer shaft. As a result, it proved to be even smoother than Japanese equivalents. The really significant thing about the V-Rod, though, is not just that it is an extremely good motorcycle, but that it is a machine that has the technology to pass any anticipated emissions regulations and take the Harley-Davidson factory well into the future.

The Early Years
1903–1920

2

Above: The bicycle ancestry of this 1905 single cylinder machine is clearly visible in the spindly frame and large diameter wheels. At this stage the Harley-Davidson company had only been going for two years, so development was still in its infancy.

Right: By 1912 the necessity for improved reliability meant that construction had to be more rugged. This included a new front fork, the frame was strengthened, and rudimentary lighting fitted. This was powered by calcium carbide, which produced acetylene on contact with water.

HARLEY-DAVIDSON MOTOR CYCLE

Model 5 "D"—7 H. P. Motor, Double Cylinder, Magneto Ignition only—Price $325.

Above: The Harley-Davidson company was one of the first motorcycle manufacturers to understand the power of good marketing. Sales catalogs such as this one advertising an early V-twin model are now highly sought after, collectable items.

Right: The riding position on these early machines seems a little strange by today's standards. This was partly due to their bicycle ancestry, and partly due to the need for weight over the back wheel, since the skinny tires provided little traction.

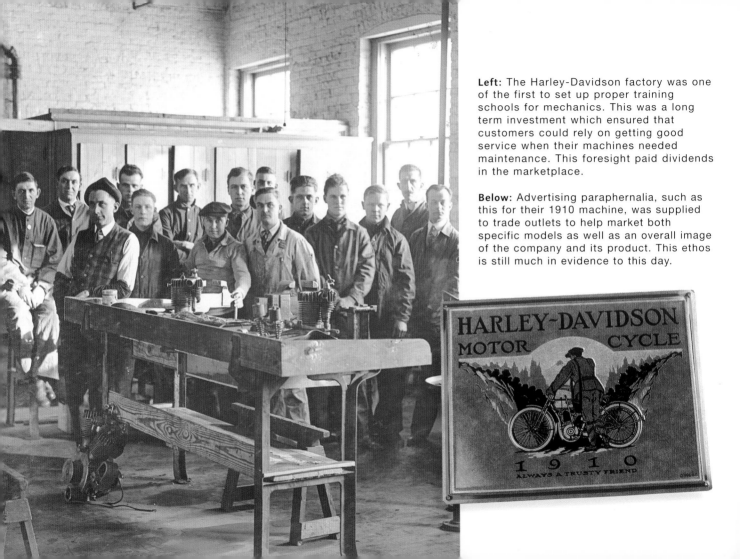

Left: The Harley-Davidson factory was one of the first to set up proper training schools for mechanics. This was a long term investment which ensured that customers could rely on getting good service when their machines needed maintenance. This foresight paid dividends in the marketplace.

Below: Advertising paraphernalia, such as this for their 1910 machine, was supplied to trade outlets to help market both specific models as well as an overall image of the company and its product. This ethos is still much in evidence to this day.

HARLEY-DAVIDSON MOTOR CYCLE

1910

ALWAYS A TRUSTY FRIEND

Above: Although mechanical reliability was continually being improved, punctures were accepted as a fact of life. This 1913 machine has a rear stand that allows the wheel to be easily removed. Many machines also came with front stands fitted.

Right: In the early days, motorcycles were expensive in relative terms—marketing material was therefore often aimed squarely at the well-to-do, such as the well-dressed young man riding an early V-twin on this advertising poster.

HARLEY-DAVIDSON

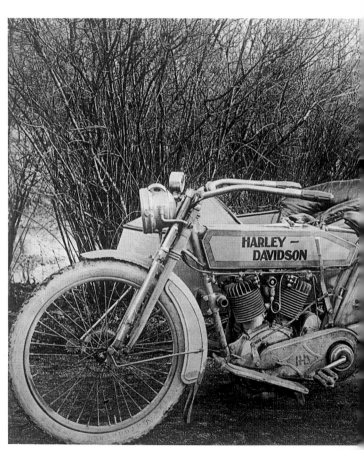

Above: Early Harley-Davidsons are few and far between these days, and command high prices on the rare occasions they come up for sale. Consequently, keeping them in top condition is a priority, for museums and collectors alike.

Right: The allure of owning a motorcycle for romantic purposes was heavily pushed in early Harley-Davidson marketing material. Here a V-twin with sidecar are shown as being ideal for taking a young lady out for a trip into the countryside.

Above: Luggage carriers, footboards, and rear brakes came as standard fitment on production versions of these machines. Many of the other parts, such as the lighting equipment were optional extras.

Right: Motorcycles were not just for the boys, as these two farm girls show with their dual seat-equipped, single cylinder machine.

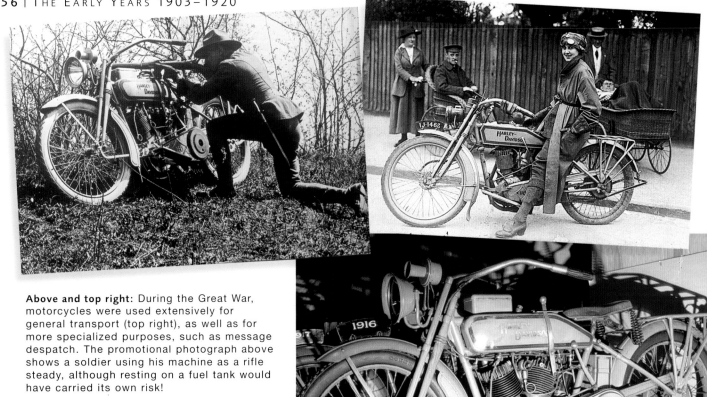

Above and top right: During the Great War, motorcycles were used extensively for general transport (top right), as well as for more specialized purposes, such as message despatch. The promotional photograph above shows a soldier using his machine as a rifle steady, although resting on a fuel tank would have carried its own risk!

Right: The hand operated gearshift lever was mounted alongside the gas tank, and the clutch was foot operated—this was also known as a "suicide clutch." Using the two together smoothly required judgment, skill, and plenty of practice.

Below: In an effort to convince prospective purchasers that sidecars were a superior form of travel, many were appointed with luxurious leather of the highest quality. The reality is that on any but the best roads, traveling in one would have been a bone-jarring experience.

Right: While belt drive had been used for many years, machines such as this 1916 Model J used chain transmission. On solo motorcycles this was an improvement—when a sidecar was fitted, however, it was vital due to the extra weight to be hauled.

Pre-War Years
1921–1940

3

Harley Legends: Model JD

The 1920s were a difficult time for all manufacturers the world over; it was the first true global recession —an economic crisis which had its roots in the Great War. Much of Europe was bankrupt, which reduced the export market for motorcycles dramatically. The search for work led many people to use motorcycles as

everyday transportation—this being at a time when automobiles were still generally only for the better off.

The 1926 Model JD shown here reflects the factory's attempts to keep costs to a minimum—paint schemes were austere, and expensive finishes such as nickel plating were only used where absolutely necessary. Design improvements continued through the lean years, however, with changes to many items including the clutch, the fenders, and the overall styling between 1925 and 1927. The engine was an F-head V-twin of 74 ci., which made a claimed 24 hp; it

Left: This Model JD shows many of the features that are distinctive of machines of the period, such as electric lighting, smaller diameter wheels, and wider tires.

SPECIFICATIONS

Engine:	F-head 45deg V-twin
Displacement:	74 ci.
Transmission:	3-speed
Horsepower:	24 bhp
Wheelbase:	59.5 in
Weight:	405 lb
Top speed:	60 mph
Original price:	$335

Right: The basic layout of all Harley-Davidson V-twins manufactured for the next few decades can be seen here on the 1926 Model JD.

had a hand-operated three-speed transmission, with both chain primary and secondary drives. The chassis was conventional, with leading link forks, and no front brake. Overall the bike was very reliable, and a good workhorse, even if performance was limited to 60 mph. At a retail price of $335, this motorcycle represented good value when compared to similar machines from rival manufacturers.

Left: If the marketing people weren't pushing the merits of sidecars for the purposes of romance, then the advantages of using them for sporting forays would do fine instead!

Below: This 1926 machine shows how the level of equipment fitted to Harley-Davidson machines had improved over the last few years. This included improved lighting, deeper fenders, electric horns, better ignition systems, and so on.

Left: As can be seen here, sidecars featured heavily in promotional material. As roads improved, so did the distance that could be comfortably covered on a day trip.

Above: Out for a run to the beach with two pretty girls! While this picture is something the marketing department dreamed up, it is also what they considered their customers aspired to.

HARLEY-DAVIDSON

Above: The top of the gas tank was a busy place! On the left was the hand-operated gearshift, and on the tank itself there were three filler caps. Two were for gasoline, and the third was for an oil compartment.

Right: While the top of the range models were all V-twins, single cylinder machines were still an important part of the model line-up. This 1927 Model BA was a utility machine aimed at the lower end of the market.

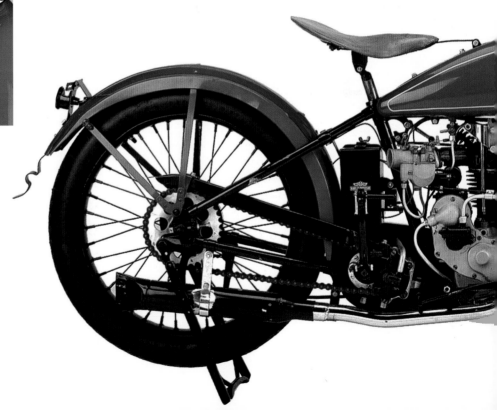

Right: This 1928 advertising poster invites the observer to compare the new models with their own machine, here derided as being a "bus," and then hopefully, to trade it against a new Harley-Davidson.

Left: A scene of contentment! Once again, a motorcycle and sidecar are shown as being occupied by a smiling, happy couple who are making the most out of their trip out into the countryside.

Left: This advertising sign boasted of a machine that returned 80 miles per gallon. While the running costs were cheap, the attraction was that the distance between fuel stops was increased—useful when supplies were far apart.

Above: The Model D was first released to the public in 1929. In the base form it featured a 45 ci. engine with low compression pistons, but a higher output version called the Model DL was also available.

Right: This advertising poster told you that Harley-Davidsons were fast, but also that they were dependable, and just what you needed in tough conditions.

At the start of the 1930s, economic hardship was still taking its toll—the stock market crash of 1929 had wreaked havoc throughout the country, and the motorcycle and sidecar provided a realistic solution to transportation needs for many families. To haul a sidecar with a full load over the rough roads of the day demanded a machine with rugged overall construction and a powerful engine with a wide spread of torque. These attributes were much more important than just having a high top speed. Simplicity of design and ease of maintenance were absolutely vital for owners who relied on their machines to travel the long distances from their homesteads and farms to fetch supplies. The VL was just such a machine (although early models had many faults)—it had a high compression version of the 74 ci. Flathead V-twin engine, and developed 30 hp at 4,000 rpm. In solo form, the VL would just about reach 80 mph, which was very good going for the day.

Above: The Flathead engine in this 1930 VL displaced 74 ci., but only produced 30 bhp. It did, however, provide ample torque to haul its 529 lb.

SPECIFICATIONS

Engine:	Flathead 45deg V-twin
Displacement:	74 ci.
Transmission:	3 speed
Horsepower:	30 bhp
Wheelbase:	60 in
Weight:	529 lb
Top speed:	85 mph
Original price:	$340

The extra mass of the sidecar meant that better stopping power was also required, and so large drum brakes were fitted to both the front and rear wheels, as well as to the sidecar wheel. All three wheels were interchangeable, which meant that if a spare was carried, it could be used to repair a puncture on any wheel. Such breakdowns were commonplace in those days.

Below: When this machine was produced, roads were still very poor. All three wheels were interchangeable, in case of punctures.

Above: This 1934 VLD came fitted with swept ends to the fenders. This became a trademark of many Harley-Davidson models that has continued to this day.

Right: The *Enthusiast* magazine was the official Harley-Davidson publication, and from the outset it did all it could to encourage women to take up motorcycling.

Opposite: The mid-1930s were a desperately tough time for the whole American economy. In order to try and stimulate sales, new paint schemes with art deco graphics were introduced to most production models.

The 1935

HARLEY-DAVIDSON MOTORCYCLES

THE 45 TWIN

This finest motorcycle of its type ever produced is the number of those who have put the 1935 Harley-Davidson 45 Twin through its paces distinguishing all the road and sound functions experience has approved over the years, this model sees incorporation a host of new advancements. Now the 45 Twin has a quickly detachable rear wheel, a new constant mesh transmission, and an efficient foot rail extending two brakes in addition to the regular front wheel brake. Three of the big 1935 improvements, like the 74 also present, genuinely dual brake cylinders, predivial headlights, single tool air intake, gas defeating muffler tool, larger valve cages, are also incorporated in this model. Five brand-new color combinations are offered for your selection. Promising swifter acceleration and much speed, easy to handle and real simple to ride, this model will prove more popular than ever with wild riders. See and ride this new 45.

THE 74 TWIN AND SIDECAR

This sidecar to take along an extra passenger to share your motorcycling joy, while one can pack his luggage or trip, and the convenience of having a quick interchangeable wheel with sidecar are some of the advantages possible with the ownership of this 74 Twin and sidecar combination. Three-point rests for safety even in this motorcycle and one on the sidecar wheel. Long wear of tire springs and deep cushioned upholstery guarantee give riding comfort for the passenger. Windshield as shown may also be had. Finished in any of the five 1935 color combinations you may select. See it at your Harley-Davidson dealer.

THE 74 TWIN

This rider who is interested in a motorcycle of great power, excellent speed, that can be ridden solo or used with a sidecar, will find his heart's desire in the 74 cubic inch Twin. For years this model has been a prime favorite with riders the world over and has been acclaimed the finest motorcycle built. Now with it gains, cast-alloy pistons, and brand-new barrel brake cylinders, it promises still greater acceleration, a easier to start, and an all-better performing machine. Front and rear wheels are quickly interchangeable and interchange alike. Wonderful riding comfort is obtained with the famous patented spring seat post and low cushioning saddle. Front and rear wheel brakes are positive and efficient. Easier brakes to boot. You oak horseshoe head brace front to rear, this model is a beauty to behold. To be had in four color combinations—the three illustrated, and also reliant green and black, and Egyptian ivory and regent brown.

THE 74 CUBIC INCH TWIN

HARLEY-DAVIDSON

THE 45 CUBIC INCH TWIN

Left: There was never any issue about equality between the sexes in Harley-Davidson's marketing material—women were always shown as being right alongside men on their own terms.

Above: This meticulously restored 1935 Model RL shows just how stylish these machines were. The two-tone paint and subtle graphics combined with flowing lines to make this a truly beautiful machine.

Above: While the look of a machine was important, function was even more so. For instance, the rear fender on this (and most other machines in the model range), was designed so that it could be folded up and out of the way in order to make removing the rear wheel easier.

In the early 1930s it became obvious to the factory that the old Flathead engine had served its time, and was due for replacement. After many trials, an overhead valve engine of 61 ci. displacement was released into the marketplace. The bike this was fitted to was officially designated as the "E," although it was not long before it became generally known as the "Knucklehead," due to the shape of the rocker covers. The first models produced suffered from various reliability problems, but the causes were soon identified by the factory and fixed. Overall, the new machine was very well received by the buying public, with the styling and paintwork being especially popular.

Power was up from the VL's 30 hp to a much more respectable 37 hp at 4,800 rpm for the "E" model, and 40 hp for the high compression "EL" version. The old three speed transmission was also replaced with a new four speed unit. All these improvements came at a cost, though—the overall weight was also increased, reaching around 600 lb. when fully gassed up. Despite the extra mass to haul around, performance was superb, with 95 mph being possible out of a good EL Knucklehead on a straight road.

Left: The Knucklehead engine fitted to the 1936 EL is considered by many to be the true grand-daddy of all the big twins' engines made by the factory ever since.

SPECIFICATIONS

Engine:	OHV 45deg V-twin
Displacement:	61 ci.
Transmission:	4 speed
Horsepower:	40 bhp
Wheelbase:	59.5 in
Weight:	565 lb
Top speed:	95 mph
Original price:	$380

Above: In an effort to minimize production costs, the exhausts were not chrome plated, but finished in flat black paint.

Left: The centrally mounted speedometer came as standard equipment on the 1936 EL. Until then, these were optional extras.

Riding the PONY EXPRESS!

HARD riders — those men of the pony express. Urging foam-flecked ponies over winding trails, "Make time" was the watchword of those daring men of other days. And "make time" is the slogan of Harley-Davidson riders today. Their tireless mounts need no urging. A twist of the throttle—and the new '35 Harley-Davidson takes you whizzing along the trail hour after hour. It's got what it takes for thrill-riding. Plenty of getaway — speed — stamina — and high-stepping style. No need longing to own one. Ask your Harley-Davidson dealer about his Easy-Pay Plans. Then have your Harley-Davidson NOW — when you want it most!

1935 HARLEY-DAVIDSON

Mail this Coupon

Reckless Speeders

—SLOW DOWN WHEN THEY SEE MOTORCYCLE OFFICERS

There is no longer any doubt about the outstanding value of having uniformed officers on motorcycles patrolling streets and highways day and night. Reduction of accidents and violations has proved to more and more enforcement departments that this method "puts the brakes" on recklessness and speeding. Why? Because motorcycles keep the officers where they can be seen—where their presence makes would-be violators unwilling to "take chances." All the more reason for mounting YOUR squads on 1937 Harley-Davidson Police Motorcycles, whose many improvements make them the ideal vehicles for fast, dependable, low-cost police service . . . . . Phone your nearby Harley-Davidson Dealer NOW—to bring over a new 1937 model for your inspection. Or write us for literature.

Harley-Davidson Motor Co.   Dept. PU   Milwaukee, Wis.

HARLEY-DAVIDSON
The Police Motorcycle

SAFETY POSTER Free!

A striking safety poster that has gained nation-wide recognition and approval. Copies free to Enforcement Departments on request. Write promptly as supply is limited.

Above left: The factory rarely missed an opportunity to link their machines with the country's heritage. In this advertising poster, a parallel is drawn between how a horse was used to warn of advancing enemy troops, and how a Harley-Davidson had become the modern equivalent.

Above right: "Reckless speeders slow down when they see motorcycle officers." This poster tells its own story!

Below: The green and silver color scheme for the paintwork on this 1936 VLH was new for that model year, as was the cover over the front fork spring. A chrome plated exhaust shows that the economy was getting stronger—customers could now afford to pay extra for such considerations.

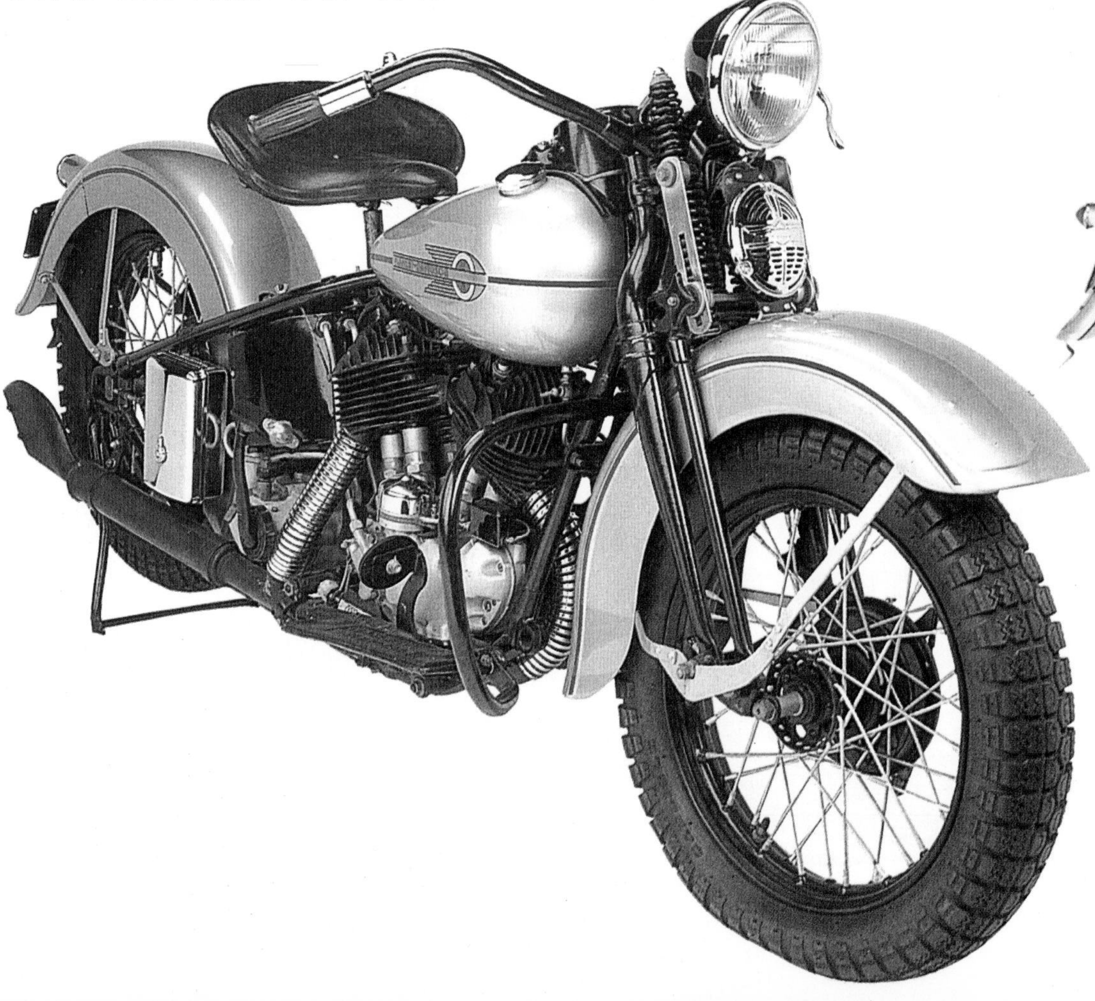

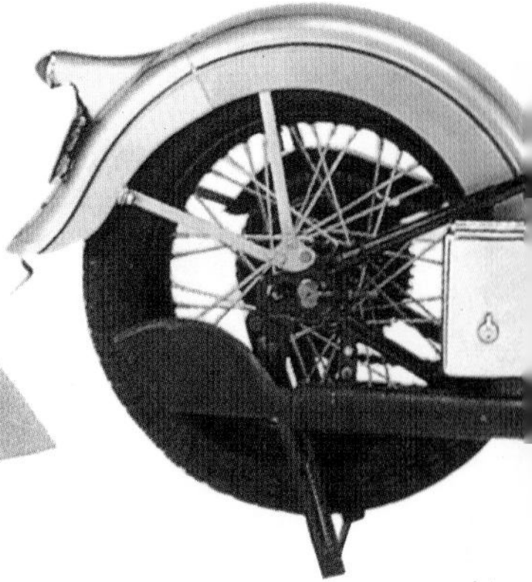

HARLEY- DAVIDSON

for 1938

The open road is calling — the magic of mountains, plain, and seashore awaits your exploration. Happy motorcycle club boys and girls welcome you to their tours and runs and invite you to take part in their good times. Back and forth to work, evening trips, weekend jaunts, vacation tours — your Harley-Davidson brings you healthful outdoor sport and economical transportation. Swing into the saddle and enjoy Motorcycling — The World's Greatest Outdoor Sport.

Opposite and above: The 1938 Model U displaced 74 ci. This made it the number one choice for those who wanted to haul a sidecar, since the extra capacity gave it a massive boost in stump-pulling torque.

Right: Once again, a clean, wholesome appearance was pushed as representative of Harley-Davidson riders. With matching "his and hers" apparel, this couple are setting off on their 1938 Knucklehead to enjoy "the magic of the mountains, plains, and seashore."

Above: This lovely machine is a 1939 EL. The Knucklehead had been in production for three years when this model was produced, and as a result it benefited from lots of small improvements, including many strengthened engine components, such as oil pump drive gears, and valve springs.

Left: This type of enameled sales sign was typical of those used at Harley-Davidson dealerships all over the world. These days they are highly sought after by museums and private collectors.

Right: The chassis also received attention as a consequence of the lessons learned from three full years of production. This included things like the use of self-aligning steering head bearings, and the centrally mounted "cat's eye" instrument panel.

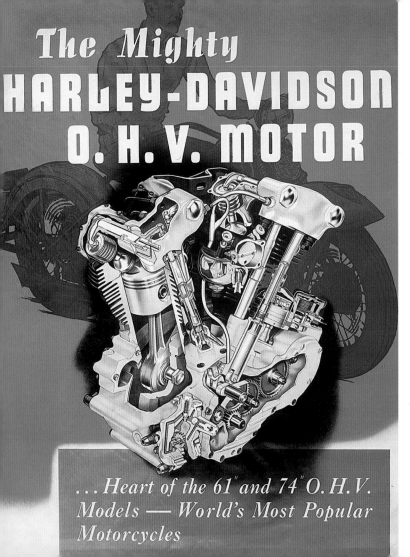

The Mighty
HARLEY-DAVIDSON
O. H. V. MOTOR

...Heart of the 61" and 74" O.H.V. Models — World's Most Popular Motorcycles

Left: This factory advertising poster trumpeted the availability of two different displacements for the OHV Knucklehead engine.

Right: This fine looking black machine is a 1941 EL Knucklehead. At this time, the whole country was gearing up for war with Japan and Germany, and so development of civilian motorcycles was more or less halted.

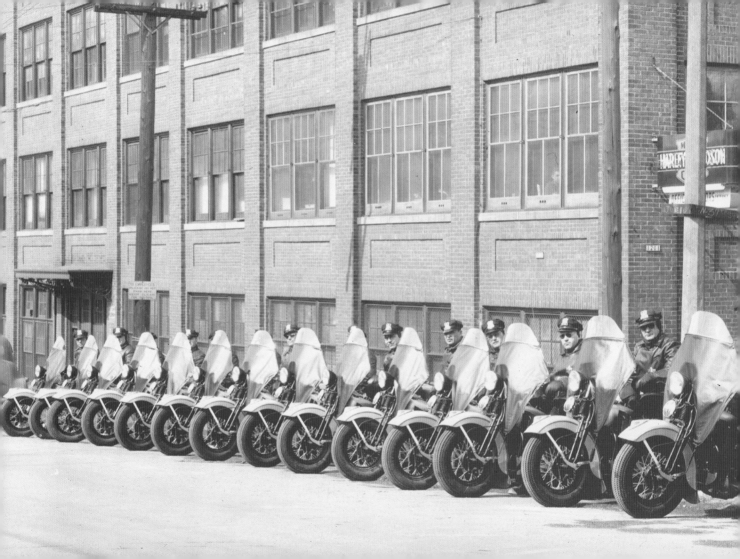

Police, Wartime, Import, and Utility **4**

The Servi-Car was originally intended for use by garages as a service vehicle for attending breakdowns and acting as a tow recovery "truck." It wasn't long, however, before many other commercial uses were found for this versatile machine. It first appeared in 1932, and was powered by the 45 ci.

Flathead engine which drove a standard type differential via a conventional three speed transmission and drive chain.

Performance of the Servi-Car was limited due to the combination of an engine which only produced 22 hp and an all-up weight of 1,360 lb—a top speed of 45–50 mph was the limit. Once the factory realized that these machines were being used for many more purposes than they anticipated, they brought out optional larger body sizes. Many police departments relied on Servi-Cars, as did all manner of other customers, from ice cream vendors to maintenance crews, and

Left: The cargo boxes, which were available in several different sizes, made these machines invaluable for everything from mail deliveries to garage service vehicles.

Right: The Servi-car was originally perceived as a model with limited appeal. However, it went on to become the model with the longest production run of all!

of course, the intended garage market. They were also popular with countless companies for making deliveries, from mailmen, to bakers, to grocery suppliers. Many purchasers painted the sides and rear of the bodywork with advertising signs, which turned them into mobile billboards.

By the time this particular model was built in 1941, many modifications had been made to the original chassis design. It had upgraded brakes, a stronger rear axle, a new frame, and a towbar had been added. The drivetrain also received many improvements, including an upgraded transmission, a better clutch, and an enclosed chain.

SPECIFICATIONS

Engine:	Flathead 45deg V-twin
Displacement:	45 ci.
Transmission:	3 speed
Horsepower:	22 bhp
Wheelbase:	61 in
Weight:	1,360 lb
Top speed:	50 mph
Original price:	$510

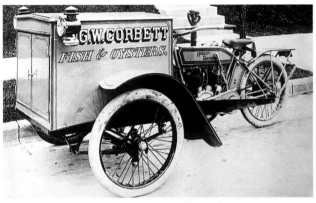

Above left: The use of motorcycles as utility vehicles dated from the earliest days—this included machines such as this vintage seafood delivery forecar.

Above: Their suitability for carrying bulky equipment made three wheelers popular with the police, fire, and other associated emergency services, as well as with civilians.

Left: When times were hard, businesses had to cut back, and the possibility of using the economical "Package Truck" to deliver goods—instead of the more expensive four wheel alternatives—made them attractive propositions.

Right: Servicars weren't all used for transporting oily car parts and acting as vehicle recovery trucks, as this advertisement shows!

Harley Legends: 1942 WLA

When war broke out in Europe in 1939, the British and their Commonwealth allies suddenly needed military equipment of every kind, including motorcycles. The Harley-Davidson factory had already been testing various prototype bikes for use by the army, who had stated that the top speed must be at least 65 mph, and that the engines must not overheat at low speeds. After the testing was completed, a bike fitted with the 45 ci. engine was selected as being the most suitable design, and thus the WLA was born. Soon after the WLA reached production, orders were received from South Africa and Great Britain for a total of 7,000 machines.

The 45 ci. engine had a compression ratio of 5:1, and developed 23.5 hp; it had a three speed transmission, chain final drive, and weighed 540 lb. This combination gave the required 65 mph top speed, but acceleration was poor

Left: With its gun pouch and olive drab paintwork, there's no mistaking the military origins of this machine.

—however, performance was far less important than reliability. Breaking down by the roadside is bad enough, but in wartime the consequences of mechanical failure can be dire. That the factory succeeded in achieving a superb military workhorse can be seen in the production figures—by the end of the war, they had produced around 88,000 military bikes, with customers including not only the western allies, but also the Russians and the Chinese.

Right: The strongly built pressed steel luggage rack was designed to carry a military radio or other similar weighty items.

SPECIFICATIONS

Engine:	Flathead 45deg V-twin
Displacement:	45 ci.
Transmission:	3 speed
Horsepower:	23.5 bhp
Wheelbase:	57.5 in
Weight:	540 lb
Top speed:	65 mph
Original price:	$380

U.S. DEPARTMENT OF THE NAVY

MOTORCYCLE, HARLEY DAVISON, 74 CU. IN.

MODEL		CAPACITY		
SER.		YEAR OF MANUFACTURE		
ENG. SER. NO.				INSP. STAMP
REGISTRATION NO. USN				
FSN		CONT. NO.		
SHIPPING WT.	LB.	GROSS VEHICLE WT.	LB.	
OVERALL HEIGHT	IN.	WIDTH	IN.	LENGTH	IN.
WARRANTY	MO. OR	MI.	DATE SHIP.	

MFD. BY

Above: As with all military equipment, every motorcycle had to have an identification plate. This one signifies that the machine belonged to the US Navy.

Left: The XA was designed to cope with war in the desert, and hence had shaft drive and a low center of gravity. After Rommel had been defeated in the sands of North Africa, there was no longer a need for this model, and it was discontinued.

Above and right: It seems a little incongruous to have a machine fitted with a 120 mph speedometer, that also has a warning plate cautioning the rider not to exceed 65 mph!

The Enthusiast

A MAGAZINE FOR MOTORCYCLISTS

DECEMBER 1942

FORT KNOX

Home of Mechanized War Specialists

BY MAJOR HENRY B. HENSON
Public Relations Officer
Ft. Knox, Kentucky

PART II

ONE mammoth chart in the school's motorcycle department illustrates the power train, tracing everything which transmits power. A huge wooden transmission, four times normal size, illustrates the gears of both the shaft-drive and chain-drive models.

Latest innovation in the department is an ingenious cut-away motorcycle model, probably the only one in the world. Assigned to the difficult task, Staff Sergeant Reese Parsons personally sawed in two every part of the motorcycle. Cylinders

When an army rider finally finishes his course at Ft. Knox, he can twist a throttle with the best of 'em.

Left: A soldier mounted on a Harley-Davidson on the front cover of the official magazine—the company didn't miss the chance to demonstrate how patriotic it was being by supplying machines for the war effort. Many soldiers learned to ride at the army's Fort Knox training center.

Below: While the XA was not far from being a straight copy of the BMW flat-twin, there were good reasons for using the same layout. Chain drive is a liability in sandy conditions, and so having shaft drive made a lot of sense. Lowering the center of gravity by using a flat engine made it easier to pick up off the floor.

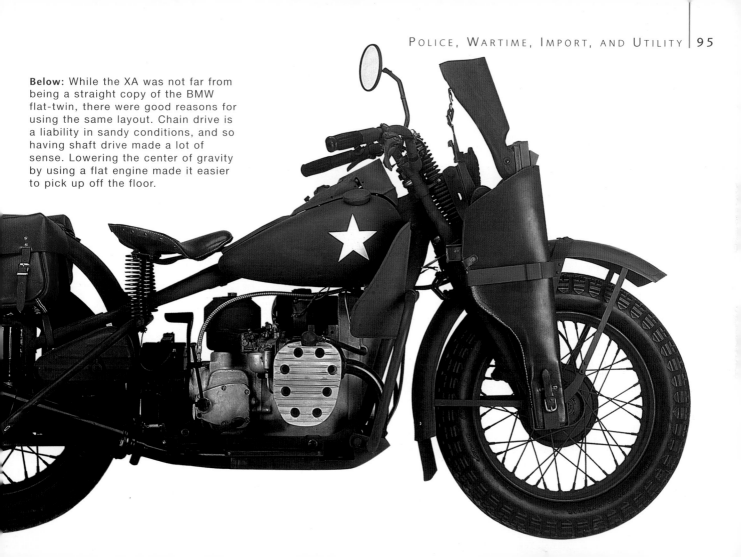

Opposite: By the time they've been painted up, it's hard to tell just by looking which of the surviving 45's were originally wartime machines, and which were built for civilian use.

Below right: It is unlikely that this 1945 WLD would originally have been supplied with so many chromed parts—the raw ingredients for plating processes were in short supply as a result of the Second World War.

Left: The cat's eye instrument panel was centrally mounted on the gas tank, and carried the speedometer, warning lights, and ignition switch.

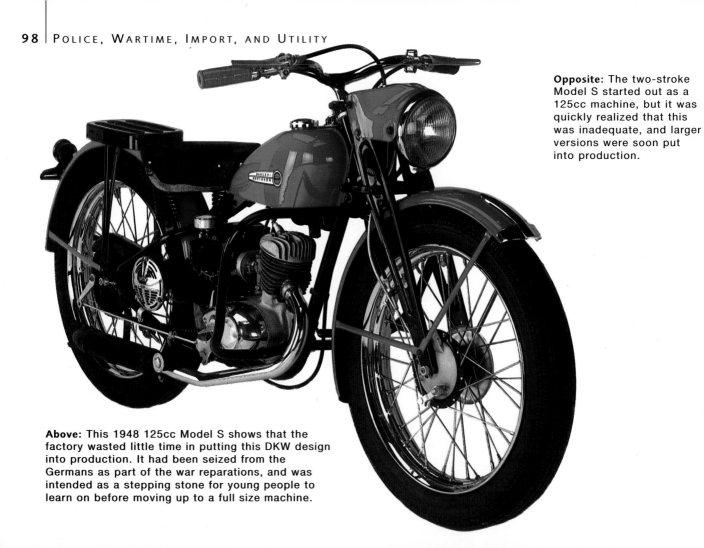

Opposite: The two-stroke Model S started out as a 125cc machine, but it was quickly realized that this was inadequate, and larger versions were soon put into production.

Above: This 1948 125cc Model S shows that the factory wasted little time in putting this DKW design into production. It had been seized from the Germans as part of the war reparations, and was intended as a stepping stone for young people to learn on before moving up to a full size machine.

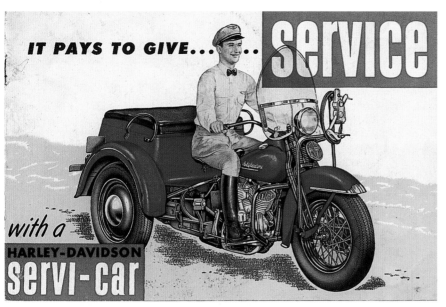

IT PAYS TO GIVE... ...service

with a
HARLEY-DAVIDSON
servi-car

Above: Initially built as a low-volume niche machine, once the factory realized how popular the Servi-car was going to be, it lost little time in promoting it to every possible market as an invaluable tool for their trade.

Right: The strange device fitted in front of the headlight is a towing clamp used to help recover broken-down automobiles.

Opposite: This 1955 Servi-Car was used as a garage service vehicle for many years before being bought and carefully restored for a private collection.

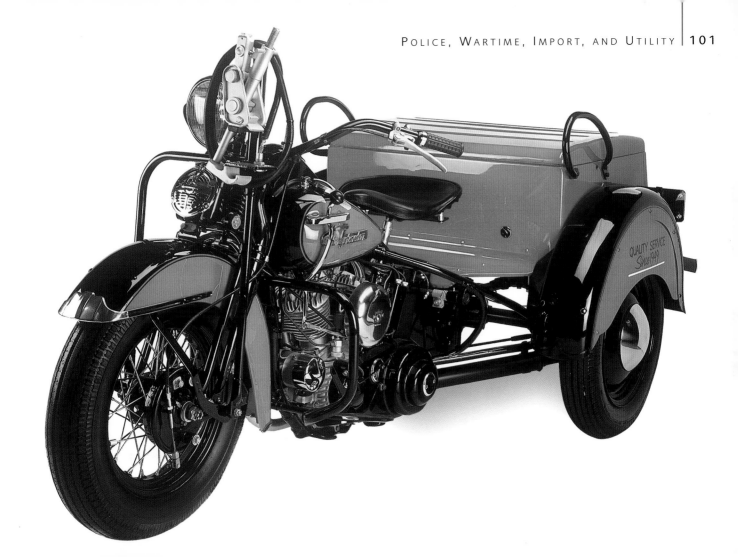

Above: Harley-Davidsons were standard issue to the police right up until the 1970s, but with reliability falling and the costs of running them rising, many departments defected to BMWs, or even worse, to the Japanese!

Opposite: The Shovelhead engine powered police machines for many years. When it was finally replaced by the Evolution Blockhead, many police departments sold off their Japanese bikes and bought American again.

Left: The Harley-Davidson factory sold its own line of lubricants, such as these oil cans. Such ephemeral items are now sought after by collectors.

Right: The Topper was the factory's answer to the flood of imported European scooters. Unsurprisingly, it missed the mark by a mile and was a complete sales flop.

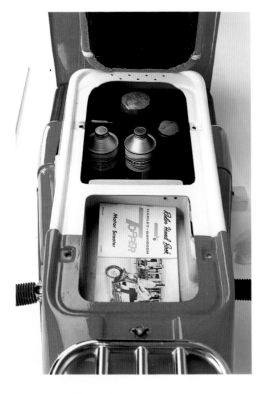

Left: Billed as an economical utility machine, advertisements for the Topper tried to promote the useful luggage carrying space under the seat.

Right: The Topper was aimed squarely at commuters and students, but it was a lost cause, and soon disappeared from the model range.

LIGHTWEIGHT... PACER 175 c.c.

Left: The 125cc Model S eventually grew into the 175cc Pacer. This provided it with enough power to be a useful commuter, or learner machine, unlike its earlier incarnation.

Below: The 1963 Scat was intended to be a dual purpose machine that could be used either on the road or as an off-roader. In order to be more suited to this role, it came with a high-level front fender and good ground clearance.

Above: The 1965 M50 was a 50cc two-stroke machine imported from Aermacchi. While it was a long way from the factory's usual products, it was a genuine attempt to compete in the marketplace with the ubiquitous Honda 50.

Opposite: "Sporting" variants of the M50 came in many guises, including larger, 65cc-engined machines. These were not much more successful in the showroom than than their smaller brethren, even with the 65 per cent power boost claimed by the factory.

Below: The Leggero was a successful machine in its native Italy, but the American public were singularly unimpressed with it and its smaller 50cc cousins. It was even less popular with the factory dealer network, who struggled to make any significant numbers of sales.

Left: Brave words indeed! While the claim that the bike was priced to meet the competition might have been true, sadly the claim that it was better engineered than its Japanese rivals is in fact highly unlikely.

Below: The 1970 Rapido ML-125S was another ill-fated attempt by the factory to compete with the Japanese. It failed to perform, either on the road or in the marketplace.

Below: This is a 1972 X-90, of a type known as a "monkey bike" to some. It had a four-speed transmission, and a 90cc two-stroke engine, and was primarily bought as a bike for teaching kids how to ride.

Below: The four-stroke Sprint SX350 was built as a direct attempt to compete with the Yamaha DT series of machines; this is a 1973 example. Unfortunately, it was too heavy, too slow, and too expensive to have any hope of achieving this, and was discontinued in 1974.

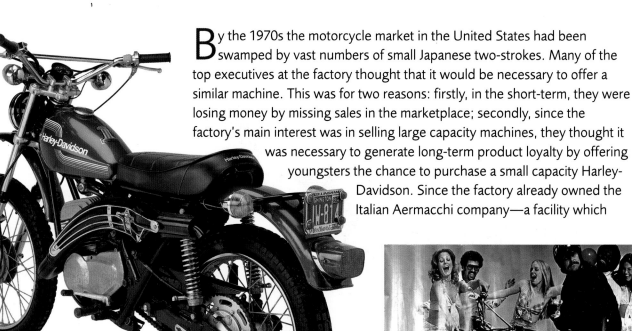

By the 1970s the motorcycle market in the United States had been swamped by vast numbers of small Japanese two-strokes. Many of the top executives at the factory thought that it would be necessary to offer a similar machine. This was for two reasons: firstly, in the short-term, they were losing money by missing sales in the marketplace; secondly, since the factory's main interest was in selling large capacity machines, they thought it was necessary to generate long-term product loyalty by offering youngsters the chance to purchase a small capacity Harley-Davidson. Since the factory already owned the Italian Aermacchi company—a facility which

Above: After the demise of the four-stroke engined SX350, the factory tried again with a range of two-stroke engined machines. This is a 1975 SX250.

specialized in building large numbers of small machines, it made sense to use their production line for this purpose.

The first two-strokes were under-powered and overweight, but by the time the 1975 SX250 pictured here was built, the power to weight ratio was about right, although they were never particularly fast. Once the initial teething troubles had been sorted out, the 175 and 250cc models sold reasonably well, and provided moderate competition for the Yamaha DT175 and DT250 trail bikes. There were two basic variants—the SS versions were for road use only, whereas the SX models were intended to be ridden both on the road and on dirt tracks. By the late 1970s, it was becoming increasingly hard to convince customers to purchase an Italian-made lightweight two-stroke, and they were dropped from the Harley-Davidson line-up.

Right: The Italian-built SX range of two-stroke road and off-road models was finally discontinued in 1978—to the relief of most dealers.

Opposite: No matter how the marketing department tried to promote the SX range of models, they failed to achieve the desired sales figures.

SPECIFICATIONS	
Engine:	Two-stroke single cylinder
Displacement:	250cc
Transmission:	5 speed
Horsepower:	18 bhp
Wheelbase:	56 in
Weight:	270 lb
Top speed:	90 mph
Original price:	$1,142

Below: When the Aermacchi factory was sold off to the Cagiva concern, it was the end of the line for Harley-Davidson's involvement with small two-stroke machines, leaving them free to focus on what they were best at—big twins!

Below: The factory tried hard to find an import that would sell. They introduced the Rapido, which flopped. They then superseded it with the TX125, but that also bombed, so they replaced it by this machine —the Z-90. Finally, they sold the Aermacchi concern back to the Italians....

Left: After years of trouble trying to make unreliable Shovelhead-engined machines suitable for use as police bikes, the Evolution engine was introduced, solving pretty well all of the problems at a stroke.

Below: These days you'd be hard pushed to find an officer who doesn't love his Harley-Davidson to bits!

Opposite: With its low-maintenance Evolution engine, superb reliability, and good performance, Harley-Davidson once again is the number one choice for most police departments.

Below: Hard luggage cases are provided as standard equipment on all police models, providing storage for bulky equipment and, of course, a radio.

Post-War
Big Twins

5

After the Second World War had ended, production of domestic motorcycles was able to get back up to speed. There was a massive market awaiting these new machines—wages earned by civilian workers in the production of war equipment, together with the back-pay of returning American servicemen, meant demand outstripped supply. The 74 ci. F series Knucklehead-engined E and EL machines were particularly popular—although the war had reduced their sales to a minimum, development had continued throughout this period.

As wartime shortages were overcome, the bikes began to have more and more parts finished in chrome plate, until they reached the standard of the late 1946 machine shown here, resplendent in its bright colors and shining metalwork. A new design of front fork was fitted—this had a hydraulic damper instead of the friction damper used on earlier models. This improved the compliance of the front suspension, and together with improved seat designs, the overall ride quality was much better.

Left: It was somewhat optimistic fitting a speedometer that read up to 120 mph on a machine that would struggle to reach 100mph!

SPECIFICATIONS

Engine:	OHV 45deg V-twin
Displacement:	74 ci.
Transmission:	4 speed
Horsepower:	50 bhp
Wheelbase:	59.5 in
Weight:	565 lb
Top speed:	100 mph
Original price:	$650

Below: This beautifully restored machine is a 1946 FL, and is equipped with many optional extras, such as saddlebags, odometer, and rear view mirror.

Above: This 1946 Model F has had many chromed parts fitted since it was produced by the factory. These include the exhaust system, the toolbox, and the air cleaner cover.

Right: This Knucklehead may be an old machine, but it's still an absolute blast to ride!

Opposite: This lovely 1946 FL has been "upgraded," like so many others, with parts, plating, and paintwork that were not available to the public so soon after the war had ended.

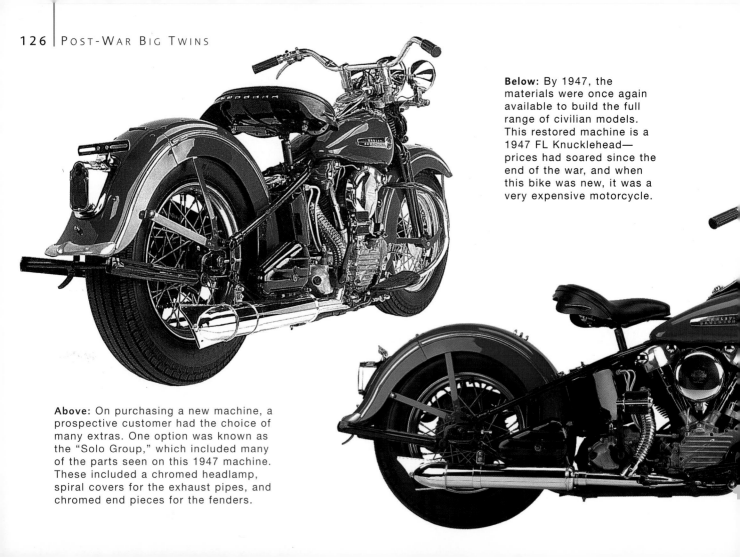

Below: By 1947, the materials were once again available to build the full range of civilian models. This restored machine is a 1947 FL Knucklehead—prices had soared since the end of the war, and when this bike was new, it was a very expensive motorcycle.

Above: On purchasing a new machine, a prospective customer had the choice of many extras. One option was known as the "Solo Group," which included many of the parts seen on this 1947 machine. These included a chromed headlamp, spiral covers for the exhaust pipes, and chromed end pieces for the fenders.

Right: When the
Panhead was
introduced to the
public it was heralded
as a new machine.
It was, however,
still basically a
Knucklehead engine,
with improved
cylinder heads.

Right: The war had
ended, and what could
be better than to
promote riding through
peaceful countryside
with a pretty girl on a
Harley-Davidson?

The Knucklehead engine was replaced in 1948 by the Panhead—so called for its pan-shaped rocker covers. This powerplant was a straight evolution from the "Knuck," and featured many improvements, including a revised lubrication system, with the external oil lines replaced by internal drillings, and a higher capacity pump to keep it flowing. These modifications really helped the Panhead engine to become established as a firm favorite with many Harley-Davidson riders—oil leaks were much reduced, and cylinder temperatures

Right: This 1950 EL Panhead has the optional Speed King leather saddlebags fitted, along with the Deluxe solo seat. Note the unusual ends to the mufflers.

were lowered due to the cooling effects of better oil distribution. This was also helped by the use of aluminum for the cylinder heads, and the fitment of hydraulic lifters—something the factory still uses to this day. These were beneficial in many ways—the valve-gear ran more quietly, since there were no longer any gaps between the lifters and the pushrods, the engine ran cooler, and no adjustment was ever needed. The changes did not effect the power output to any great extent, but reliability was much improved.

The 1950 EL Panhead shown here is a DeLuxe model, with extra chrome trim, including engine crash bars and fender protectors. The most significant feature of this bike, however, is that it has the factory's first fully hydraulic front end, which were known as "Hydra-Glide" forks. It was at this time that the range of optional extras was considerably increased to cater for the wishes of owners who wanted to personalize their machines. This was a milestone in the ethos of the Harley-Davidson company, and it certainly helped the marque to survive to the present day.

Above: The Duo-Glide was introduced in 1958, and was so-called because it had hydraulic suspension at both the front and rear ends of the bike. This gave a much improved ride.

SPECIFICATIONS

Engine:	OHV 45deg V-twin
Displacement:	61
Transmission:	4 speed
Horsepower:	45 bhp
Wheelbase:	59.5 in
Weight:	590 lb
Top speed:	90 mph
Original price:	$650

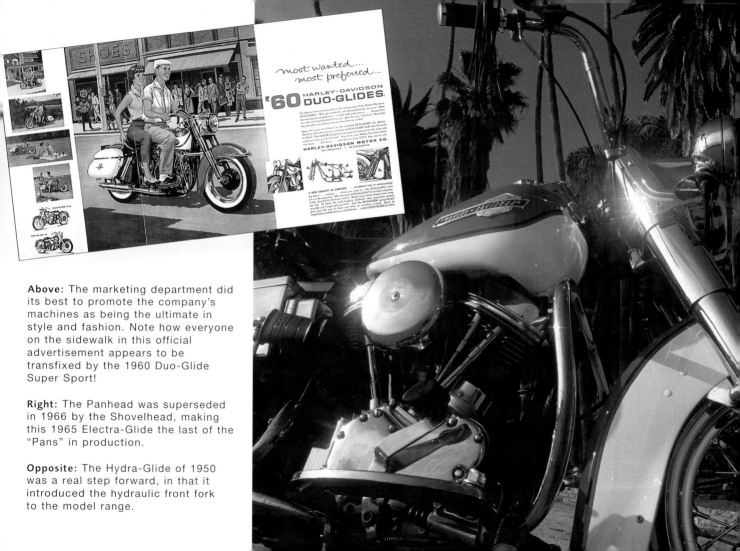

Above: The marketing department did its best to promote the company's machines as being the ultimate in style and fashion. Note how everyone on the sidewalk in this official advertisement appears to be transfixed by the 1960 Duo-Glide Super Sport!

Right: The Panhead was superseded in 1966 by the Shovelhead, making this 1965 Electra-Glide the last of the "Pans" in production.

Opposite: The Hydra-Glide of 1950 was a real step forward, in that it introduced the hydraulic front fork to the model range.

Left: The Electra-Glide was so named because it introduced an electric start to the factory's line-up for the first time. The tombstone speedometer was named after the shape of the region under the speedo needle.

Opposite: When it was built, this 1965 Panhead Electra-Glide was the ultimate in refinement and style. Machines like this are now highly sought after by private collectors.

Harley Legends: FX Super Glide Boat-tail

By the end of the 1960s, there were two basic choices if you wanted to buy a new Harley—you could have an overweight, slow, and cumbersome Electra-Glide, or you could have the boy racer's Sportster. There was no middle ground, and so many potential customers instead bought a second-hand machine, and stripped off all the unnecessary parts to create their own interpretation of what they thought suited their needs. Although the Harley-Davidson factory was going through all manner of internal disputes at the managerial level, there were still a few who recognized that a whole market was being missed by the failure to offer a middle ground machine. As a result of this realization, in 1971 the FX Super Glide was born—the "F" signified the contribution of components from the FLH, and the "X" came from the use of Sportster parts.

By this time, the Shovelhead motor had progressed from using the old generator cases from the Panhead, to having its own improved bottom end, which became known variously as the "cone-motor," or as the "alternator Shovel." The Super Glide was basically a stripped-out Electra-Glide with a Sportster front end. The machine pictured here had a fiberglass rear fender, which soon got nicknamed the "Boat-tail"—it was not popular with

Left: The first of the Super Glide range was available with an optional fiberglass "boat tail." While the bike was very popular, the seat unit was not.

SPECIFICATIONS

Engine:	OHV 45deg V-twin
Displacement:	74 ci.
Transmission:	4 speed
Horsepower:	55 bhp
Wheelbase:	62 in
Weight:	560 lb
Top speed:	110 mph
Original price:	$2,500

Below: The Super Glide range remains popular to this day, although when it was first produced, many questioned its existence.

customers, and was quickly dropped from the model range and replaced with a more conventional, though stylish, steel item. The Super Glide was a massive milestone in the history of the Harley-Davidson factory—it is debatable if the company could have survived without the success of this iconic machine.

Below and opposite: Harley enthusiasts are resourceful people, and when the factory produced badly built machines, they just took them apart and rebuilt them the way they wanted them. Here we see such a machine—a beautifully constructed Shovelhead, with shotgun pipes, rigid rear end, and eye-catching paintwork.

Above: This 1977 FXS Low Rider had the misfortune to be produced at a time when the factory was experiencing all kinds of difficulties. Morale was low among the workforce, and there were rumors of deliberate sabotage; both reliability and sales suffered as a result.

Left: The dash layout of the 1979 FXEF shows the tachometer mounted below the speedo. Quite why it goes as high as 8,000 rpm, though, is a mystery!

Above: Although most of the top brass at AMF Harley-Davidson remained aloof from the reality that the majority of their customers were "bikers," rather than "enthusiasts," those such as Willie G. realized that a machine like this FXEF would appeal to large numbers in the marketplace.

Above: The 1980 FXB Sturgis was fitted with a new electronic ignition system. Some riders threw it away and re-fitted contact breakers, because they figured that while a mechanical system may need more maintenance, at least it can be fixed at the side of the road.

Right and above right: The FXB used a toothed belt as final drive, instead of the usual chain. The belt was quieter, lighter, needed less adjustment, and gave a smoother ride. If a stone or other road debris got caught under the belt, however, it could break without warning. If this happened, emergency repairs were not simple, and as a result many people have been left stranded at the side of the road far from home.

Left: Sometimes you may see two bikes that are very similar. These two beautiful custom Shovelhead chops are not just similar—with the exception of the seats, they are pretty well identical!

Opposite, left: The machine on the left has a dual seat fitted, whereas the other has a solo seat. Other than that, these two immaculate machines could have come off the same production line, except that they are clearly the work of dedicated customizers.

Opposite, right: Just about every nuance has been replicated, from the spoked wheels to the location of the speedometer, making these bikes as close to a true pair as you can get!

A big year for the factory in many ways, 1984 was the end of the line for the Shovelhead, and the beginning of production of the Evolution engine was a massive step forward. There were other advances, too, including the release of the Softail; this was designed to look as though it had a rigid rear end, just like a chopper, when in reality it had fully operational suspension hidden under the transmission. The retro look had arrived, and it proved very popular in the marketplace—something that the factory has capitalized on ever since.

Left: Designed to look like a rigid, the Softail actually has two shock absorbers cleverly hidden under the transmission.

The Softail was effectively a Wide Glide with a different rear end, although it had a whole host of other features added, including forward controls, a kick start lever, a 21 inch front wheel, and a new two-piece seat. The combination of a new rear end, a larger front wheel and lots of rake meant that this was the longest machine in the line-up, with a massive wheelbase of over 63 inches. It rode well enough though, and the new Evolution engine was an instant success. This was developed in conjunction with Ricardo Engineering in England; it had excellent oil control, and exhaust emissions were low thanks to the efficiency of the unusually shaped combustion chambers.

Apart from the cylinder heads, the Evolution engine was ostensibly similar to the Shovelhead—however, there were very few shared components. Almost everything was revamped, from the connecting rods which had ten times the fatigue life, to the oiling system which was vastly improved. The new cylinder heads were topped off with three piece rocker boxes (although the prototype only had two), and due to its squared-off shape, the engine was soon nicknamed the "Blockhead." The multi-piece construction allowed the engine to be serviced without having to remove it from the chassis. All in all, the Blockhead was a fine engine, and it powered the Big Twin range for years to come.

Below: The Evolution engine was more than a Shovelhead with a new top end. It was a major re-design, and marked a re-birth of the company's fortunes.

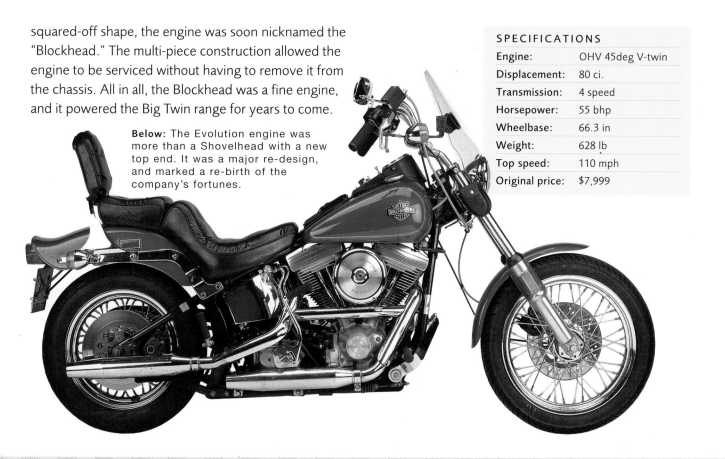

SPECIFICATIONS	
Engine:	OHV 45deg V-twin
Displacement:	80 ci.
Transmission:	4 speed
Horsepower:	55 bhp
Wheelbase:	66.3 in
Weight:	628 lb
Top speed:	110 mph
Original price:	$7,999

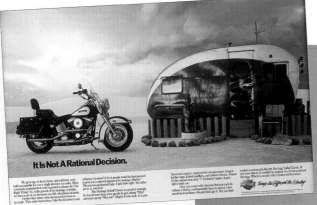

It Is Not A Rational Decision.

Above: By the late 1980s, private ownership had made its mark, as can be seen by the adverts put out by the marketing department, who now knew how to speak directly to the market without misjudging or insulting them.

Right: This machine belonged to the late Brandon Lee, who was accidentally killed while making a feature film.

Opposite: An Aladdin's cave of Harley parts! Who knows what treasures lie hidden under a bench or behind a pile of parts?

Harley Legends: FXRS

The FXR and FXRS variants of the Super Glide were born early in the 1980s—they were superficially similar to the FXs, but had five speed gearboxes and compliant mountings for the powertrain, instead of the four speed transmissions and solid mounts of their brethren. It was not long before these acquired the nickname "rubber-mounts." At this stage they still had Shovelhead engines, but by the time the machine pictured here was built, these had been superseded for the much improved Evolution Blockheads.

Belt final drive replaced the conventional chain and sprockets—this was much smoother, required less adjustment, and no lubrication. This was a significant improvement until such time as some road debris found its way between the pulleys, when the belt would tend to snap with no warning. While this would often leave the owner stranded, it also meant a major strip-down would be required to fit a replacement, since the swing-arm had to be removed to get the new belt on.

The Evolution FXRS was not a great performer in stock form, since it only produced 55 bhp. Not many remained unmodified for long, however, since they responded so well to simple changes. The stock air cleaners were deliberately restrictive, as were the mufflers—this was to ensure that the bikes would pass the strict emissions regulations stipulated by

Left: The FXRS was a real rider's machine—built for those who wanted to take in the miles without windshields and panniers. This gorgeous bike is a 1988 example.

government agencies. Some owners simply rammed a steel bar up each muffler to knock the baffles out of the way, others just bought aftermarket parts. Either way, the bike immediately sounded better, and gained a significant power increase. Likewise a replacement air filter would replace the stocker—after this a new camshaft and carburetor generally made an appearance.

Depending on the technical expertise or wealth of the owner, all manner of other modifications could be made, including ported heads, higher specification valves, high power ignition systems, and so on. It was possible to extract well over 100 bhp with the right modifications—much more than the chassis was designed to handle. The FXRS was thus a capable and versatile machine which came as a sort of blank canvas onto which the owner could add his or her own touches.

Above: The FXRS changed little over the years— it didn't need to! Detail improvements, however, meant that refinements continuously crept in here and there.

SPECIFICATIONS	
Engine:	OHV 45deg V-twin
Displacement:	80 ci.
Transmission:	5 speed
Horsepower:	55 bhp
Wheelbase:	63 in
Weight:	580 lb
Top speed:	110 mph
Original price:	$11,999

Opposite: The Fat Boy was such a success that it became a style icon of the 1990s—every movie star who wanted to be "seen" bought themselves one and went cruising the boulevards and highways of fashion.

Above: With its disc wheels and solid look, the Fat Boy was a wholly original design concept. Once again, it came from the inventive mind of Willie G. Davidson, demonstrating that the large amounts of time he spends at rallies and shows is well-spent. He gets to understand what the market actually wants!

Harley Legends: Fat Boy

When Willie G. Davidson designed the Super Glide in the early 1970s, he set the way ahead for many years, producing a machine the customers had been crying out for, if only the factory would listen. Later in the same decade he came out with the XLCR, which was more of a design exercise than a revolution. He followed this up with the XR1000 in the early 1980s, which was another example of styling brilliance. While he has been responsible for all manner of other machines, these three models stood apart as separate entities. How could he have followed them up with something as innovative and stylish at the same time? Well, the Fat Boy was his answer to that dilemma! He blended the Softail Custom with the Heritage Softail Classic and came up with the Fat Boy, designated the FLSTF. Somehow this machine also blended

SPECIFICATIONS	
Engine:	OHV 45deg V-twin
Displacement:	80 ci.
Transmission:	5 speed
Horsepower:	55 bhp
Wheelbase:	62.5 in
Weight:	665 lb
Top speed:	110 mph
Original price:	$10,995

modern looks with a retro feel. It was an instant hit, with large numbers being built from the outset. But why was it such a success? Well, rumor has it that this is the machine Willie G. built for himself, and as he is a very keen rider, racking up more miles than most of his customers could dream about, he knew just what it would take!

Left: Stock mufflers don't usually last long once the bike has left the showroom! Both the sound and power output can be vastly improved with the fitment of aftermarket items.

Opposite: The Fat Boy is not just for looking at, it's for riding, too. Here a fortunate individual has the chance to cruise through the hills on a sunny day. What could be better?

Opposite: The retro-meets-future design of the Fat Boy is so clean that you have to look twice to make sure that all the components are really in place.

Right: With its oil-tight cases and unrivaled reliability, the Evolution engine really makes a bike like this.

Below: The Fat Boy has understated paintwork and graphics, because that is all it needs.

Left and far left: The speedometer and surrounding dash panel could have come straight out of the 1950s, as could the headlamp and smoothly streamlined nacelle. This combination of retro styled parts and modern technology has helped create a machine that could only have come from the Harley-Davidson factory.

Opposite: This view is as American as apple pie on Sunday—a peek past the handlebars of this Fat Boy reveals the Harley-Davidson factory behind.

Opposite: It looks as though this rider on his Heritage Softail Classic is trying to wring a little more speed from his machine. If so, he's either in a hurry, or has missed the point of what life with a bike like this is all about....

Above: People who ride Harleys generally like to hang out with other Harley riders—it's a given thing! Not only are such people able to meet up with their own kind, but they can check out each other's machines at the same time.

Left: This emblem is one of the most recognizable product symbols to be found anywhere in the world. It cleverly utilizes the eagle, which immediately establishes it as being American, and when combined with the name Harley-Davidson, and the statement "Made in USA," it needs no further introduction.

Opposite: This machine looks right at home posing against a sky background. It is a 1993 FXWDG Dyna Wide Glide, with raked out forks, a 21-inch front wheel and Wide Glide triple trees.

Above: Evel Knievel used to be one of the most famous people in America. He was a daredevil who broke just about every bone in his body during his career of jumping buses, bridges, and just about anything else he could find—on a motorcycle!

Above right: A Harley-Davidson gas tank and a cowboy hat with motorcycle goggles—how all-American is that?

Opposite: Two Harley Softails, two riders, and plenty of desert to travel through. Life just couldn't get any better....

Opposite: Here's a view over the clocks and through the handlebars of the Capitol Drive buildings which form the headquarters of the Harley-Davidson Motor Company.

Below: The FXDS Dyna Convertible is a dual purpose machine—the windshield and saddlebags can be removed very quickly, allowing the rider to choose between long distance tourer or bar-hopper.

Opposite: This late model Softail is known as the Bad Boy. Whilst being very similar to the Fat Boy, it has a different front end from the Springer Softail. This particular example has had many other parts fitted, including a sprung seat, and loud pipes.

Above: Some people don't modify their machines very much after they purchase them, although even this Low Rider has had a few small additions.

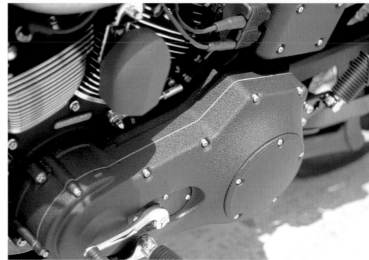

Above: The primary side of the Twin Cam looks very similar to that of the earlier single cam model.

Left: It is easiest to recognize the Twin Cam engine from the right hand side of the bike, where the distance between the lifter blocks is a sure give-away. The addition of an extra cam is one of the few ways in which it was really possible to improve the design of the Evolution engine.

Opposite: The new Twin Cam engine displaces 88 cubic inches, giving it an immediate boost in torque and horsepower. This 2000 FXDX is fitted with a version of the new engine which uses a 40mm CV carburetor, whereas other models use sequential-port fuel injection. This motorcycle also uses twin balancer shafts in the motor to reduce vibration, making it more suited to long distance riding.

Harley Legends: V-Rod

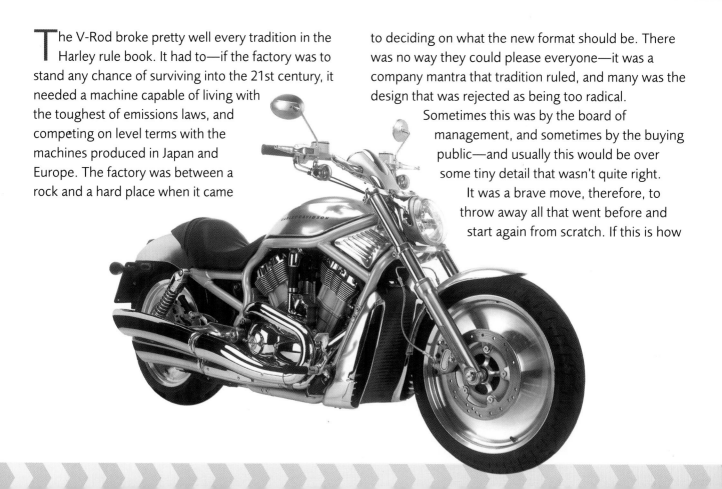

The V-Rod broke pretty well every tradition in the Harley rule book. It had to—if the factory was to stand any chance of surviving into the 21st century, it needed a machine capable of living with the toughest of emissions laws, and competing on level terms with the machines produced in Japan and Europe. The factory was between a rock and a hard place when it came to deciding on what the new format should be. There was no way they could please everyone—it was a company mantra that tradition ruled, and many was the design that was rejected as being too radical.

Sometimes this was by the board of management, and sometimes by the buying public—and usually this would be over some tiny detail that wasn't quite right. It was a brave move, therefore, to throw away all that went before and start again from scratch. If this is how

SPECIFICATIONS

Engine:	DOHC 60deg V-twin
Displacement:	69 ci.
Transmission:	5 speed
Horsepower:	115 bhp
Wheelbase:	67.5 in
Weight:	615 lb
Top speed:	135 mph
Original price:	$16,995

Opposite: The V-Rod marks one of the biggest changes in design philosophy the factory has ever experienced.

Right: This cutaway engine reveals that there are no components that are shared with the Evolution series. About the only thing in common is that it has two pistons.

it appears though, it was not quite the reality, since the V-Rod engine was actually derived from that used in the VR-1000 racer. This gave it some—if limited—genuine Harley-Davidson heritage. Like the racer, this engine was a liquid-cooled, 8-valve V-twin, disposed at 60 degrees. Unlike it, however, the displacement was 1130cc, and it featured a contra-rotating balance shaft as well as rubber engine mounts to more or less eliminate vibration.

The resulting machine is a thoroughly modern motorcycle, quite unlike anything that is being produced by rival companies. The general styling is distinctive, and not to everyone's tastes—it is, however, most definitely a Harley-Davidson.

Left: Riding a V-Rod is like riding no other motorcycle, especially any previous Harley-Davidson. It handles, it stops, but most of all, it really goes!

Opposite: It is quite clear that when this motorcycle was designed, it was not on just a clean sheet of paper, but on a new drawing board, as well.

Left: Lorum ipsum dolor sit amet conse ctetuer adipis cing elit, nommy nibn euismod tincy ut laeret bulor mange.

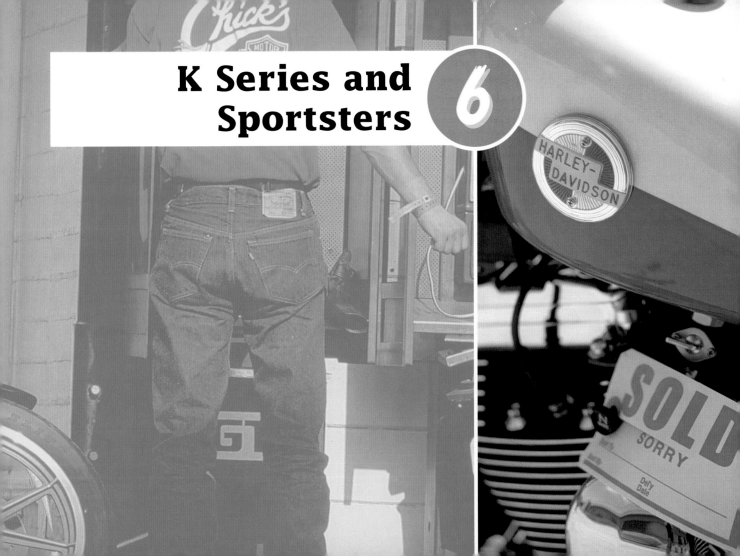

K Series and Sportsters

6

The Flathead format continued to be represented in the Harley-Davidson model range in a new engine designed to power a series of 45 ci. machines. These were intended to compete directly with the large numbers of European imports, and were thus equipped with foot operated gear shifts, and hand clutch levers.

Another departure from the norm was the use of hydraulic suspension at both the front and rear.

Unfortunately, although the "K" model featured all these technical advances, it weighed over 400 lb—since the engine only developed 30 hp, it was ruined by very poor performance. To make matters worse, it was more or less incapable of coping with the added load of a passenger. The factory's short-sighted justification for this was that they believed their customers were very traditional, and that designs with too many new

Left: A great song and dance was made by the factory when the K was introduced to the public for the first time.

SPECIFICATIONS

Engine:	OHV 45deg V-twin
Displacement:	45 ci.
Transmission:	4 speed
Horsepower:	30 bhp
Wheelbase:	56.5 in
Weight:	400 lb
Top speed:	80 mph
Original price:	$865

Below: While the 45 ci. K Model was not a success, it was a vital stepping stone towards the creation of the Sportster.

features would be rejected. The disappointing sales figures of the K model caused by the mediocre power output meant that it was soon realized that major improvements were needed, and so it was discontinued in this form after only two years, with a total of less than 4,000 machines being produced. The racing version of this engine, known as the "KR," however, went on to achieve considerable success in its time.

Above: The 1954 models of the KH carried an emblem on the front fender commemorating the 50th anniversary of the Harley-Davidson company's foundation.

Right: The KH was basically a K model with a longer stroke—this brought the displacement up to 55 ci. The extra capacity gave the bike a lot more torque, which gave better performance, but also a lot of broken transmissions.

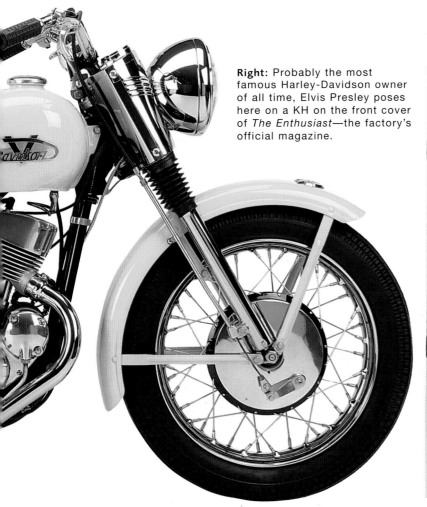

Right: Probably the most famous Harley-Davidson owner of all time, Elvis Presley poses here on a KH on the front cover of *The Enthusiast*—the factory's official magazine.

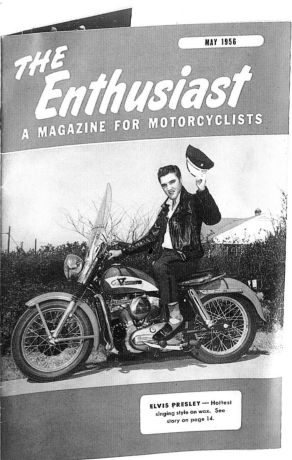

MAY 1956

THE Enthusiast

A MAGAZINE FOR MOTORCYCLISTS

ELVIS PRESLEY — Hottest singing style on wax. See story on page 14.

Harley Legends: KHK

When the K model was discontinued, it was replaced by the KH, which was fitted with a larger version of the same engine. The modification was achieved by increasing the stroke, and the capacity went up from 45 ci. (750cc) to 55 ci. (883 cc). It was also fitted with larger valves, and an improved four speed transmission—these changes made a significant difference to the machine's performance, especially to the torque delivery.

Unlike its predecessor, it was now more than capable of carrying a passenger. It was claimed to make 38 hp, and this made it two seconds quicker in the quarter mile than the K, with the top speed being in the region of 95 to 100 mph.

In 1955, the KHK was released. This was a high performance version of the KH, and featured a factory fitted kit of parts including a roller bearing crank, sports profile camshafts, and

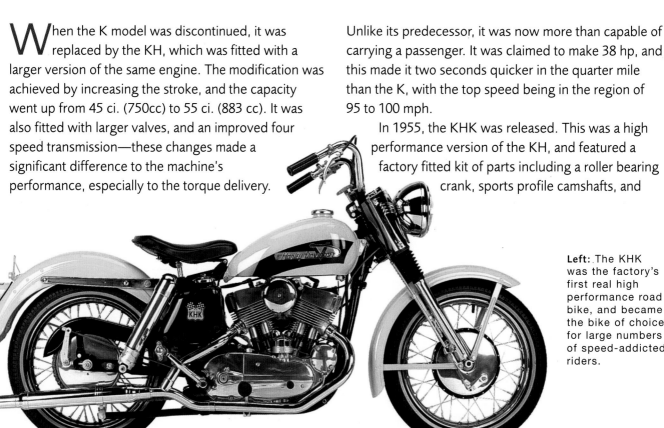

Left: The KHK was the factory's first real high performance road bike, and became the bike of choice for large numbers of speed-addicted riders.

ported cylinder heads. This model became a hot rod legend, and while it was meant to be a supplement to the KH range, it actually outsold it in the showrooms. The popularity of such machines was noticed by the top brass at the factory, who had previously believed that the public were more interested in dependability than performance. This change of heart led directly to the creation of the Sportster range.

SPECIFICATIONS

Engine:	OHV 45deg V-twin
Displacement:	55 ci.
Transmission:	4 speed
Horsepower:	40 bhp
Wheelbase:	56.5 in
Weight:	440 lb
Top speed:	100 mph
Original price:	$1,003

Above: The KHK was available in stock form or with an optional factory-installed high power engine kit.

Harley Legends: *XL*

The release of the Sportster was a milestone in the history of the Harley-Davidson company. Initially called the "XL," it was more or less a KH with overhead valves, although the long stroke crank was replaced with a shorter throw item and the bore was increased. This was done for several reasons—while the lower piston speed allowed more rpm, the larger bore size also permitted bigger valves to be fitted. A lower piston speed also resulted in reduced oil consumption, due to better piston ring sealing.

The XL chassis was very similar to the KH series, and although it came equipped with a solo seat, a dual version could be ordered as an optional extra. Other official accessories included saddlebags, a windshield, and many smaller items. The machine pictured here is a 1957 model, which makes it from the first year of production—these were fitted with a 7.5:1 compression ratio engine, which made about 40 hp. In 1958, the XLH model was given 9:1 pistons, and at the same time a further increase in valve size was implemented, making the power around 45 hp. Performance was excellent for the time, and demand was high in the marketplace. For the first time in a long time, this allowed the factory to compete with the vast numbers of European imports on its home soil.

SPECIFICATIONS	
Engine	Ohv 45deg V-twin
Displacement	55 ci. (883cc)
Transmission	Four-speed
Horsepower	40 bhp
Wheelbase	57 in
Weight	495 lb
Top Speed	105mph (169kph)
Original Price	$1,103

Opposite: The XL Sportster was more or less a KH with overhead valves. The overall package was, however, something that added up to more than the sum of its parts.

Left: The XL Sportster was sprung on an unsuspecting public in 1957, opening up a whole new chapter in the factory's history.

Left: The top brass at Harley-Davidson were determined to keep the image of its product as clean and wholesome as possible. As a consequence, its marketing material always depicted customers as being happy, smiling, and successful people, as can be seen here in this promotional image.

Opposite: The XLCH carved out something of a reputation for itself as a hot rod motorcycle, even in box-stock form straight out of the showroom. A stock XL made in the region of 40 horsepower, whereas as this mean machine delivered 55!

Opposite: Sportsters, like many other models in the range, could be ordered with all sorts of different components. This XLCH has the small gas tank and solo seat options fitted, although they may well have been changed since the bike was new.

Above left: One of the problems with a lot of the earlier Harley-Davidson models is that the carburetor sticks out of the right hand side—just where your knee wants to be. However, most owners eventually find a riding position that suits them.

Above: The early Sportsters had beautiful lines, something that the design staff at the factory are still only too well aware of. A comparison between a 1950s XL and a modern Sportster shows that the adage "If it ain't broke don't fix it" has been well heeded at Harley-Davidson....

Harley Legends: *XLCH*

The success of the Sportster created a demand for yet more performance, and when in 1958 a group of California dealers placed an order for sixty machines—the minimum number the factory would agree to produce—the

XLC was born. This was a stripped-out version of the Sportster, with no battery, no lights, straight-through exhaust pipes, and a smaller gas tank. It was instantly a success, with many people using these machines for unofficial street drag racing; these events were highly illegal, but extremely popular. Once word got around about the XLC, demand was so great that the factory produced the XLCH.

Left: The look of the late 1950s XLCH was so popular that it set the scene for Sportster styling for the next four decades. The original look has been lost on this machine which has had a custom seat and sissy bar fitted.

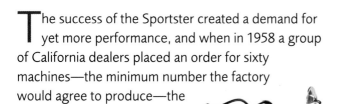

SPECIFICATIONS

Engine	Ohv 45deg V-twin
Displacement	54 ci.
Transmission	Four-speed
Horsepower	55 bhp
Wheelbase	57in
Weight	480lb
Top Speed	120mph

Most XLCHs came equipped with a single seat, small tank, and magneto ignition—although the list of optional extras was vast, and included such things as alloy wheel rims and high-level exhaust pipes. Even in this lightened specification, the bike was still heavy, weighing in at about 480 lb. The power output of a

Above: Sadly, the beautiful lines of this XLCH have been ruined by the fitment of a custom seat that belongs on an entirely different kind of bike.

standard engine was around 55 hp. In stock form, the XLCH would pull around 14 seconds in the quarter mile, and had a top speed of about 120 mph.

Above: By the time this machine was built in 1964, the XLCH had become the bike to beat at drag strips all over the country. Backyard tuners did all they could to find even more power than the factory provided, and the better ones made these bikes really fly.

Above and right: This machine—an XLH from the 1966 model year—was the last of the kickstart-only Sportsters. Since these often had carburetor problems, it is no surprise to see that there is an S&S air cleaner fitted to this bike. It almost certainly means the stock carb has been replaced in favour of a high quality S&S unit. This would have given better gas mileage, better starting—especially on cold mornings—and much improved performance.

In 1967 the Sportster was modified to receive an electric starter; in order to power it, a bigger battery was also fitted. The paybacks were that it cost more to produce, and the bike got quite a lot heavier.

Right: The machine shown here is a 1971 XLH Sportster. This model differed from the XLCH, in that it was more of a generalized road bike than a hot rod.

Right: The XLH's larger gas tank gave it a better range than that of the XLCH, and most examples had a dual seat fitted. Other than that, by the 1970s these models were very similar.

Below: By 1974 Sportsters came equipped with a disc front brake and a 61 ci. engine—up from the previous 55 ci. While the official factory figures suggested that the horsepower output remained the same, the torque delivery was certainly better, and as a result acceleration improved.

Above: A variety of official Harley-Davidson spray paint products typical of the day. From heat resistant paint to straight colors, the factory was only too keen to manufacture such items for its customers to purchase.

Right: Being a patriotic company, it was only natural that the American bicentennial was celebrated by Harley-Davidson. This poster was one of the methods they used to promote the idea. It shows the four founders of the company in association with the words "The Great American Freedom Machine, 1776–1976."

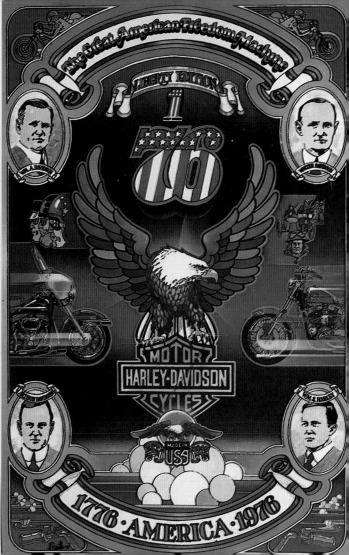

Harley Legends: XLCR

By the late 1970s, Japanese superbikes dominated the motorcycle market the world over—they offered high performance at a relatively low price, and sold well. The Harley-Davidson factory knew it was in trouble, and did what it could to tempt customers into the showroom. One such project involved the XLCR—the Café Racer—a name which harked back to the days when unofficial road races were held between English cafés by do-or-die enthusiasts on stripped down sports bikes.

The XLCR was a beautiful blend of flat track styling and contemporary Sportster components; it had the 1000cc XL engine, special exhausts finished in flat black, a stretched rear fender like the XR750, a handlebar fairing, a new frame, and gloss black paintwork highlighted here and there with areas of polished alloy. It was a masterpiece of styling, and was probably well ahead of its time, but all the same was a failure in terms of sales, and was dropped from the 1979 model range.

Right: The XLCR was a factory design exercise, but all the same, the overall style of this machine was entirely down to the pen of Willie G. Davidson.

The main failings of the XLCR were simply that although it looked fast, its performance just did not compare with that of its competitors. It was slow, it didn't handle, and it was too heavy—at a time when Japanese and Italian machines would top 140 mph, the XLCR struggled to manage 110 mph. While the bike did not live up to its promise, it was partly responsible for the introduction of better components to the Sportster range, and as a design exercise for the styling department, can be considered to have been a great success.

SPECIFICATIONS

Engine	Ohv 45deg V-twin
Displacement	61 ci.
Transmission	4 speed
Horsepower	68 bhp
Wheelbase	58.5in (1511mm)
Weight	515lb
Top Speed	115mph

Left: The 1977 XLCR was one of the prettiest bikes to come out of the factory in many years. It was inspired by the beautiful lines of the XR750 racers.

Below: This pretty 1979 XLH has had several changes made to it over the years. The paint on the gas tank and fenders is not original, and neither are the exhaust pipes and mufflers.

Above: A set of AMF-era spark plugs, contact breakers and condenser form an ignition system maintenance kit, prominently marked with the words "Harley-Davidson Genuine Parts & Accessories."

Right: This logo is unusual in that the "AMF" lettering is bigger than that for "Harley-Davidson." However, this odd imbalance did not last long....

Left: The Harley-Davidson Motor Cycles logo is one of the most recognizable on the planet, and is probably worn in the form of patches, pins, and tee shirts by more people than any other in the world.

Opposite: Some custom bikes are wonderful creations. This one appears to be a wonderful creature!

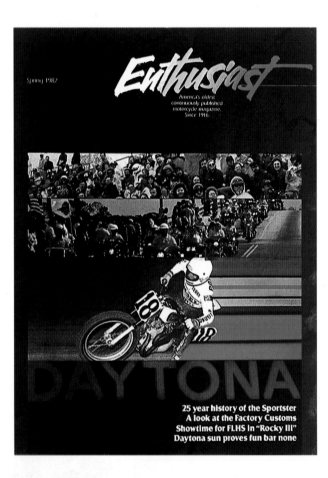

Left: This issue of *The Enthusiast* magazine—with the front cover showing Scott Parker performing gymnastics on an XR750—had a feature covering 25 years of official Sportster history.

Right: This 1982 XLH Sportster was a special 25th anniversary model with limited edition paintwork in black and silver. About 1,700 were produced out of a total Sportster production of around 8,000.

Above: The factory produced official items depicting the eagle emblem for many years. Such memorabilia are very sought-after by collectors these days, with some of the rarer ones fetching large sums at auction or in private sales.

Left: The 1983 XLX. Now that it was back in private hands, the Harley-Davidson company went from strength to strength, with vastly improved employee morale being but one example. As a result, the quality of the bikes produced went up dramatically.

Opposite: The XLX Sportster was an excellent-looking machine. Customers thought that a price of less than $4,000 was excellent too, and good sales figures helped put the new version of the company back on its feet.

While the Big Twins got the Evolution engine in 1984, the Sportster range had to wait until 1986 —it was worth waiting for, though. The chassis it was installed in was, however, still the same as used on the old XL. The first Evolution Sportster displaced 883cc, and shortly after an 1100cc version was released, as pictured here. This was basically the same engine, but with a larger bore, and bigger pistons. The combustion chambers were markedly different to those used in the Big Twins, which had a "squish shelf" to create turbulence to improve efficiency and lower exhaust emissions. The Sportster engine lacked this feature, but due to its shorter stroke and higher compression ratio, it instead revved higher, which made it more efficient. Both engines also

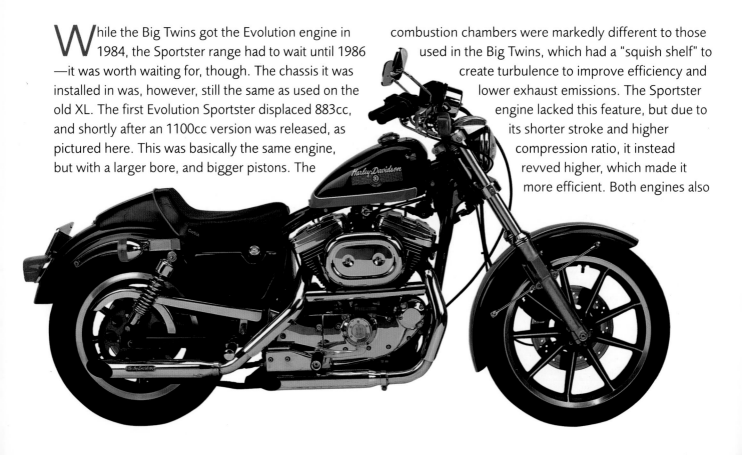

used lightweight cast alloy pistons with flat tops—this improved the thermodynamic efficiency, which reduced fuel consumption and emissions still further.

The XL-1100 developed about 63 bhp, which coupled with a weight of nearly 500 lb gave it brisk, if not particularly impressive, performance. The handling was reasonably good, and the styling was excellent. This meant that the various models of the Evolution Sportsters were very popular with the buying public, and it was—and still is—a very popular part of the factory line-up.

Right: The orange and black paint, together with the black and chrome engine, signify that this is a limited edition model.

Opposite: 1987 was the 30th anniversary of the Sportster line-up, and as a celebration of this, 600 of the 4,618 machines built were completed as special models.

SPECIFICATIONS

Engine	Ohv 45deg V-twin
Displacement	1100cc
Transmission	4 speed
Horsepower	63 bhp
Wheelbase	60 in
Weight	492 lb
Top Speed	112 mph
Original Price	$5,199

Left: The reputation of the Sportster engine as a hot rod powerplant really suffered as a result of the stifling emissions regulations imposed on it. Reliability problems experienced during the AMF era made matters worse. When the Evolution Sportster engine came along, the situation improved dramatically, especially with the 1200-engined models.

Below: This 1988 XLH 1200 Sportster has been tastefully modified using aftermarket parts, including the belly pan, and Corbin seat. The subtle and carefully co-ordinated paintwork enhances the bike enormously.

Left: The 883 Sportster was more or less the same as the 1200, with the exception of the size of the pistons and the volume of the combustion chambers. For those who wanted the extra capacity without trading up, modifications to hike the displacement were relatively straightforward.

Opposite: The stock air cleaner is usually considered to be a waste of space by most owners, since it saps power and looks mediocre. This lady appears to think otherwise, though—in this case, the chrome is acting as a handy roadside mirror!

Below: The XL1200C Sportster Custom was introduced in 1996. This bike filled a gap in the market for those who wanted a lightweight machine that had some of the appeal of the big twins. It was ideal for those with shorter legs, or those who lacked the strength to handle a larger machine.

Right: A rack of Sportster engines at the factory awaiting their turn to reach the assembly line.

Opposite: This late model 1200 shows off the low stance of the Sportster—a key factor in its popularity over the years. The factory has deliberately targeted several models at women, making them one of the few manufacturers to realize that women ride bikes, too!

Above: The Evolution Sportster has a clean, tight, and reliable powerplant. The transmission is housed in the same cases as the engine, and since its inception has been offered in 883, 1100, and 1200 forms.

Opposite: The nameplate on the gas tank of this 1200 Sportster is a retro style, harking back to the late 1950s, when the first XLs were produced.

Right: The Sportster has always been a narrow bike, and as can be seen here, this example is no different. The small frontal area helps performance, and the lack of width helps with maneuvering in traffic. The lack of bulk also translates into a lighter overall package.

Left and right: When the new owner of this bike gets it home, he—or she—is going to have to do lots of polishing if the bike is going to stay this shiny.

Opposite: This XL1200 Sportster is a good example of where the factory got to in the late 1990s with the smaller end of the model line-up. It is a clean functional machine that sells well, and for all the right reasons—there is plenty of choice in the marketplace, but people still buy Sportsters because they like them.

Right: What more can you say? This bike has already been sold. Sorry!

Sports Bikes

7

Above: The Sprint H was more or less exactly what the Aermacchi factory had been producing in the late 1950s when the Harley-Davidson company first spoke about buying them out. In other words, this 1965 machine was already five years out of date when it went on sale.

Opposite: The Sprint H 250cc was powered by a four-stroke, flat, single-engined engine, and was categorized as a street scrambler. It had a high-level exhaust, canister air cleaner, and produced about 25 bhp.

Left: The SS 350 was actually quite a good motorcycle. It had enough power to make it useful on the street, and as long as the electrics were kept dry, it was reasonably reliable.

Above: Unsurprisingly, the factory always recommended the use of its own lubricants! These days the empty cans are keenly collected by private Harley enthusiasts and museums alike.

Left: The Baja 100 was built as a scrambler, and was named after a famous motocross race held on the Baja Peninsula. Its two-stroke engine had a five-speed transmission and developed around 12 horsepower—not bad for only 100cc.

Above: The MX250 was introduced in 1976 in an attempt to cash in on the popularity of motocross and other off-road sports in the 1970s. Unfortunately, the factory's development was way behind the times, and it was completely uncompetitive on the track.

The XR-1000 was another attempt at marketing what was really a design exercise. Customers had been begging for a street version of the XR750 ever since it first hit the race-tracks in 1969, and eventually in 1983, 14 years after they were first asked for it, the buying public finally got what they wanted. However, just to show how fickle the market can be, they failed to buy it.

The miserable sales figures were due primarily to the excessively high price—at just short of $7,000 it was $2,000 more than the cost of a regular Sportster. The cost could be justified if you took into consideration the specification—the XR-1000 had special cylinder barrels, cylinder heads, connecting rods, twin carbs, and special exhausts. Manufacturing short runs of special parts costs a lot of money, even for a factory, and when a large amount of hand finishing is needed as well, it becomes prohibitive. The bike did perform, though—it made it into the 12 second bracket in the quarter mile,

which made it the fastest production Harley ever built. The incredible acceleration was thanks to its 70 bhp power output. All in all, the XR-1000 was a fine looking motorcycle, with good performance, but expecting the public to pay $2,000 more than the cost of a stock bike for an increase of only 10 bhp was too much to ask.

SPECIFICATIONS	
Engine	Ohv 45deg V-twin
Displacement	61 ci.
Transmission	4 speed
Horsepower	70 @ 4800rpm
Wheelbase	59.5in (1511mm)
Weight	465 lb
Top Speed	125mph

Right: The XR1000 was built as a design exercise that would also test the engineering skills of the development team.

Left: The engine was born out of the XR750 racer, with alloy cylinders and heads, twin carbs, and twin high-level exhausts.

Left: This machine is a Buell RR1200, which was one of a small number of machines built using the Sportster engine, but housed in a sports chassis, and enclosed in race-style bodywork. Later versions were less enclosed.

Right: Erik Buell—who started the Buell company—was in fact an ex-Harley-Davidson engineer. He wanted to see a true sports Harley in the marketplace, so he started his own company and produced one. And then he made another, different model. Eventually the Harley-Davidson factory decided to get in on the action, and bought a share in the Buell company.

Left: This Buell was built by Motown racing as a performance road bike. It features distinctive graphics and a loud color scheme.

Right: A look from the front end of the bike reveals that it has a lightweight tubular steel frame that leaves the Sportster engine in full view for appreciative onlookers. The ribbed underside of the lower triple tree also shows that low weight is a priority on this machine.

Above: Unusually for a Harley-Davidson powered machine, the speedometer on this bike is marked up to 140 mph, most of which it is capable of using.

Above: There's no mistaking who's stable this machine came from!

Above: A close-up of the front wheel shows that this Buell has been equipped with six-piston calipers, and fully floating disc rotors.

Opposite: A flush-fit racing style filler cap on the gas tank shows that this bike is indeed aimed at a sports market.

The VR 1000 project was a genuine attempt by the Harley-Davidson company to recreate past road racing glories by building a machine capable of competing in various superbike championships. The rules, however, required that they be based on production road bikes, and so the factory had to build a minimum number of 50 of these in order to take part. The engine was entirely new—it was still a V-twin, but it was arranged at 60 degrees to give enough room for the downdraught intake system to fit.

With a displacement of 1000cc, it had four valve heads, Weber EFI fuel injection, an integral five-speed transmission, and a dry clutch. It was said to produce 135 bhp, and while this was far more than any factory-produced machine ever managed, it was still not enough to compete successfully. The initial prototypes used a Harris Performance frame built in England, but production units were fabricated in the United States in an attempt to brand the machine as being entirely

Left: A view from the rider's perspective shows that the VR1000 has very little in the way of instrumentation apart from a Stack competition-derived tachometer.

SPECIFICATIONS

Engine	DOHC 60 V-twin
Displacement	61ci
Transmission	5 speed
Horsepower	135 bhp
Wheelbase	55.5in
Weight	390lb
Top Speed	170mph
Original Price	$49,490

constructed from parts that were made in America. This resulted in a lot of unnecessary development work, since many of the components were not race-proven, and initial results were certainly hampered by this strange decision. Ultimately, many unsuitable parts were replaced with genuine competition items from other countries, such as the Ohlins forks used on the road bikes.

The results did not come, even with top-level ex-GP riders

such as Doug Chandler and Miguel Duhamel. This was partly due to a lack of power, and partly because of inadequate handling. Sadly, the machine never received the development it needed to be competitive at this level, and so it soon disappeared from view.

Right: The VR1000 was built as a homologation special to allow the factory to enter superbike racing; sadly, it failed to deliver on the race tracks.

Harley Legends: Buell S1 Lightning

The Buell company was started by an ex-Harley-Davidson employee called Erik Buell. He wanted to see an all-American sports bike, and started out by building small numbers of Sportster-based machines. Eventually the top brass back at Milwaukee decided that it would be a good thing to be a part of this, and in 1993 they purchased a 49 per cent interest in the Buell company.

The Buell S1 Lightning pictured here was released in 1996. It featured a hot rod version of the Sportster engine which produced 91 bhp. Some liked it—others didn't. Foremost amongst the criticisms was the issue of the exhaust system; it looked like it came off a truck, and many Buell customers replaced it with a performance item before they even rode the bike. Another strange component was the air cleaner. This looked like a briefcase had been bolted onto the side of the engine, and yet again, most owners quickly

Left: With 91 bhp, the Buell S1 Lightning was the most powerful Harley-Davidson engined machine ever sold, when it hit the streets in 1996.

threw it away and fitted a smaller, neater unit. One thing is for sure —these ungainly items would not have been fitted if the regulations had not forced the Buell company to do so.

Nevertheless, the S1 Lightning was a good performer, and would do the quarter mile in about 12 seconds—far quicker than the stock Sportster could manage. While this machine may not be to everyone's tastes, and reliability has been an issue, many owners are very happy with their bikes.

Right: The upside-down front forks, six-piston brake calipers, and large diameter disc rotors showed that the Buell was a serious machine.

Above: The Buells were starkly different from anything else available on the market. This alone made them attractive to some prospective purchasers, but many were put off by the enormous air cleaner and truck-like muffler required by Federal emissions regulations.

Left: The underslung rear shock absorber is mounted under the transmission, and is operated by a series of rods and levers. The Sportster engine is tightly wrapped within its steel tube frame.

Right: The instruments are mounted above the upper triple tree, and tell the rider all he needs to know. The lettering on the gas tank says all that the onlooker needs to know; "Buell—American Motorcycles."

Opposite: The Buell was designed to be ridden, and ridden hard. This rider is doing what he can to live up to that requirement.

Right: The Buell X1 was fitted with an advanced fuel injection system which continuously monitors the air pressure and temperature, as well as various engine conditions, to ensure that the fueling is always spot on. This improves the performance of the engine as well as overall fuel economy.

Above: Sports riders just love to ride together—both for the cameraderie as well as the competition. These two Buell riders are making the best possible use of a beautiful evening.

Right: The Buell XB9R has many advanced features, including rim-mounted front disc rotors, giving the maximum possible braking torque. The rider of this machine appears to be taking these components for a thorough evaluation!

Racers **8**

Opposite: Sitting on the start line is always an anxious time for a racer, but the riders of these three vintage machines appear to be as relaxed as it is possible to be under the circumstances.

Above: The front racing plate of this XR750 tells a whole story on its own. Firstly, it's Number 1, which tells us that this rider is a winner. Secondly, it's covered in dirt, so it has just finished a race. And thirdly, it's on an XR, so however well it performed, it looked good.

Right: In his time, Mert Lawwill was a top dirt track rider.

FIRST AT OMAHA

Otto Ramer, riding his stock Harley-Davidson twin, took first place in each of the four events he entered at Omaha, July 4th.

The races were held over a course laid out from Fairacres to Fifty-second and Dodge Streets.

According to Omaha newspapers young Ramer climbed hills like a streak and distanced his competitors by thirty feet at every goal.

In two events Mark Schwerin finished second, also riding a Harley-Davidson.

HARLEY-DAVIDSON MOTOR COMPANY

Producers of High-Grade Motorcycles for More than Twelve Years

Milwaukee, Wis., U. S. A.

Above: When a Harley-Davidson won a race, the factory was quick to capitalize on any glory to be gained!

Right: Machines like this beautiful board track racer command enormous prices on the rare occasions when they come up for sale.

Opposite: The early board track racers were really tough. They had next to no safety equipment, and scant regard was given to their (often short) lives by the event organizers.

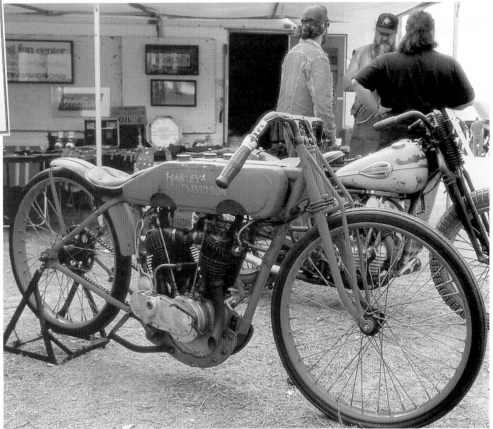

The Harley-Davidson factory's racing team first appeared in 1914, and consisted of five riders on Model 11K racers. Although much valuable advertising was gained from their racing activities, the factory wanted complete control over who had access to their competition machines. In order to dissuade privateers, they priced their racers at around five times the cost of rival marques. The Model 11K featured a 61 ci. (1000cc)

engine, which had direct chain drive to the rear wheel. While this would normally be a reliable feature, the first time the factory team competed, they were robbed of a maiden win by a stretched chain. This event was a 300 mile endurance race, and although an 8-valve Indian won, all the Harley-Davidson riders finished, and so much interest was generated that the factory pressed ahead with development of improved machinery.

The technical developments that resulted from building better competition bikes soon appeared on road machines; this not only gave them better performance, but improved their reliability as well. This was at a time when many owners used their motorcycles to travel great distances over very poor, and generally

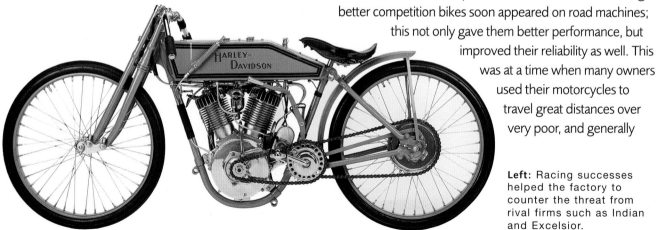

Left: Racing successes helped the factory to counter the threat from rival firms such as Indian and Excelsior.

Above: Models like this early racing machine were used by the factory to generate beneficial headlines in the press.

unmade, roads. Better dependability was a great selling point, a fact that was not lost on the marketing department, who made much of any competition successes, and continued to do so for several decades thereafter. The

Model 11K was therefore largely responsible for the factory's perception that winning races resulted in increased sales of road machines, and thus spawned a competition lineage that it still alive and well today.

Right: The factory eight-valve racers were the epitome of high-performance engine design in their day. The factory wanted to keep them out of privateer hands, and so priced them at such a ridiculously high level that no-one could afford to purchase one.

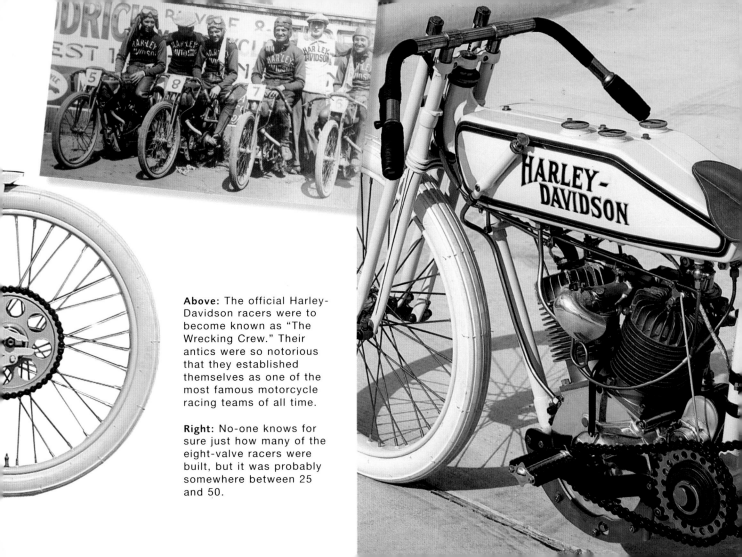

Above: The official Harley-Davidson racers were to become known as "The Wrecking Crew." Their antics were so notorious that they established themselves as one of the most famous motorcycle racing teams of all time.

Right: No-one knows for sure just how many of the eight-valve racers were built, but it was probably somewhere between 25 and 50.

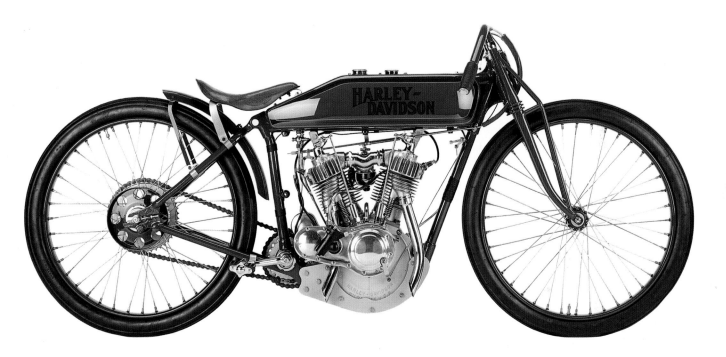

Opposite: This crew look pleased, and they have every reason to—they have just broken a speed record in their 1920 eight-valve powered sidecar.

Above: The engines of the early racers were so finely detailed that they looked like watch mechanisms. This FCA racer had a twin-cam pocket valve engine that was highly competitive in its day.

Harley Legends: 8-Valve

This machine is a 1923 eight-valve racer. Such bikes were uncompromising to say the least; they were stripped of all unnecessary components, and had no brakes, very rudimentary exhausts, little concession to comfort, and had to be started by using a tow rope. In order to reduce wind resistance to improve performance, the seat and handlebars were mounted as low as possible, to allow the rider to crouch down out of the airstream.

Left: This 1923 eight-valve racer is basically just engine and wheels—everything that can be removed has been sacrificed to save weight.

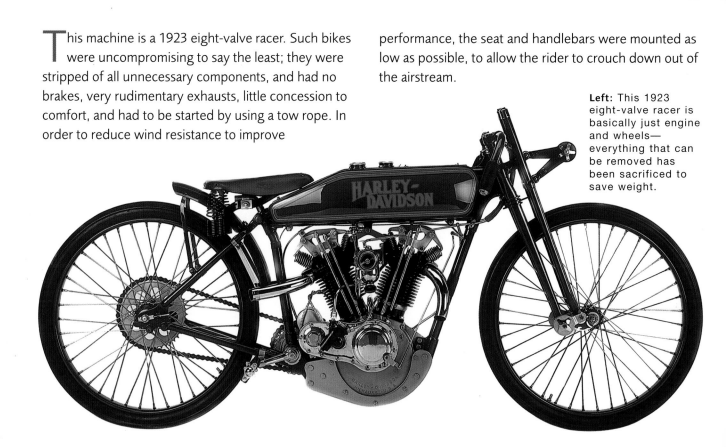

The interest generated by the factory's involvement in racing had meant the competition machines had to be continually developed in order to beat those of rival companies such as Indian and Excelsior. Early experiments with eight valve engines were very promising, and Harry Ricardo was brought in from the UK to further develop them. He was an English engineer who was the leading internal combustion expert in the world; after many weeks work, he was able to achieve a figure of 55 hp, which was incredible for the day.

The first eight-valve engines featured a single camshaft, but in 1919 these were superseded by an updated version with two camshafts. These went on to power a series of machines which, together with their simpler pocket-valve stable-mates, went on to dominate domestic competition for several years. In 1921, for instance, the factory won every National Championship in the United States. Nowadays, these exotic machines are highly sought after, and consequently command very high prices.

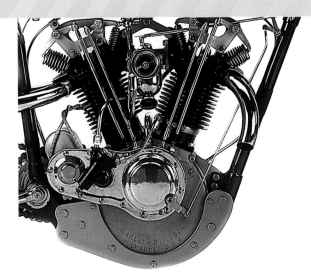

Above: The eight-valve racer used a 90 degree included angle between the valves, which were operated by exposed push rods.

SPECIFICATIONS

Engine	Ohv 45deg V-twin
Displacement	61 ci.
Transmission	Direct
Horsepower	15 bhp
Wheelbase	51.5 in
Weight	275 lb
Top Speed	115 mph
Original Price	$1,500

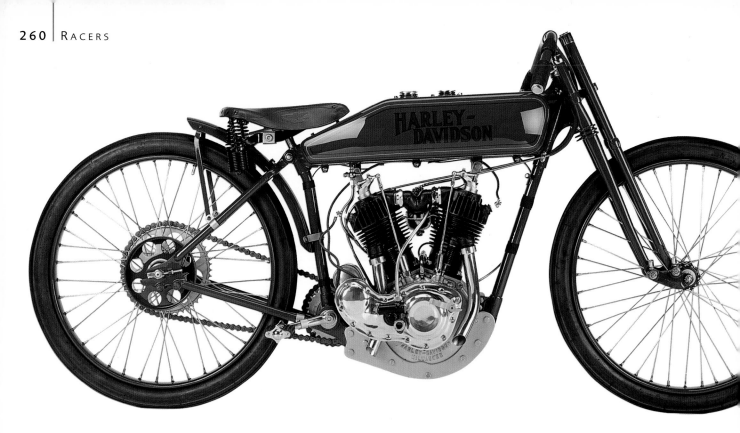

Above: This race bike was designated as the FHAC—it used a pocket-valve engine. Lessons learned by the engineers from running such machines were put to good use when later road bikes were developed.

Right: This gorgeous machine is a 1932 Model DAH which the factory produced expressly for use in hillclimbs. It used overhead valves, ultra short exhaust pipes, and the rear tyre was wrapped with chains to give the maximum possible traction in the dirt.

Right: Hillclimbs were a popular form of motorsport at a time when "proper" race tracks were too expensive to construct, or so few and far between that not many people had access to them. Hillclimbs though, cost nothing to build—any handy, and preferably dangerous, steep dirt hill would do!

Championship
Motorcycle Hillclimb
SUNDAY, MAY 8th
Eight Miles North of San Fernando on New Ridge Cut-off

SANCTION NO. 2039
American Motorcycle Association
Under Auspices of
Los Angeles Motorcycle Club

A. F. VAN ORDER   FLOYD CLYMER   PETE KEMP
Committee in charge

Right: Dirt tracks took over when board track racing declined, and are still popular to this day. This poster is advertising an event at a state fairground —such venues were often chosen for these events.

MOTORCYCLE RACES

NATIONAL CHAMPIONSHIPS
STATE FAIR TRACK
MILWAUKEE
AUG. 1 - 1926 - 2 P.M.
SANCTIONED UNDER A.M.A.

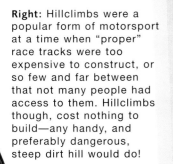

Opposite: This action shot of a competitor clearing the top of a hillclimb shows that his safety equipment basically consisted of a token helmet and some boots. It is small wonder that so many people got seriously injured.

Right: The rider here was famous in his day—Jack Seamans poses for a photo on his DAH hill-climber in 1937. Note that this is the clothing he competed in!

Left: Dirt track racing was (and still is to a certain extent), a low-budget affair. Riders often worked on their own machines, as well as driving the tow car between races—sometimes this involved covering enormous distances. The smart ones teamed up and shared the driving to events.

Opposite: The 45 engine was modified for racing, and while quite heavy in comparison to the competition built by Indian, it was more reliable. This model was designated the WLDR, but did not come with the chromed frame that is a feature on this bike.

Right: All racers love to win trophies. This one was awarded for the "Main Event" to a rider called H. Reno on August 27, 1938, by a club that called itself the "SBMC."

The WR engine was brought out in 1941—although it was derived from the "W" range of road bikes, the "R" signified that it was for racing use. It was developed to compete head to head with the latest Indian Sport Scout machines, and was freely offered for sale to customers. By this time the factory had realized that helping privateer racers was a cheap and effective way of achieving competition success, and so selected riders would receive assistance, or even the loan of complete machines. Two basic variants were produced—the WR was for flat track racing, and the WRTT for TT steeplechasing and road racing. These differed mostly in the construction of the frame—the TT version used a WL frame with many of the brackets and lugs removed, whereas the WR had a lighter and stronger frame that was specially made from chrome-moly tubing.

For marketing purposes, the engine was ostensibly the same as fitted to the WL road bikes; however, this was actually far from true—the special steel crankshafts used were just one of many internal changes made. The best WR engines, built by private tuners, made about 40 hp.

Left: The WR750 was one of the most successful racers the factory ever produced. Even years after it should have been completely out-classed, it was still winning races.

Left: This is a modern graphically-enhanced speedometer which has been retro-fitted to the KR racer shown below. It uses buffalo and feather motifs, which are native American Indian symbols.

Opposite: For some inexplicable reason, this lunatic is riding a 1950s Duo-Glide in an enduro—surely the most unsuitable machine of the era that anyone could have contemplated entering in such an event?

Below: This lovely machine is a 1956 KR racer, of which it is thought less than 500 were built over its fifteen year production life.

HARLEY-DAVIDSON

WINS BIG at SACRAMENTO, CALIF.
★ **CARROLL RESWEBER** FIRST in
25-MILE NATIONAL CHAMPIONSHIP
★ **Ron Emmick** Wins 10-Mile Amateur Race
HARLEY-DAVIDSON SWEEPS 6 OF 9 EVENTS
JULY 19, 1959

HARLEY-DAVIDSON WINS
20-MILE NATIONAL CHAMPIONSHIP

TAKES 4 OUT OF FIRST 6 PLACES

CARROLL RESWEBER-FIRST
NEW RECORD TIME:
14 MINUTES, 5.12 SECONDS

JOE LEONARD -SECOND

BRAD ANDRES -FOURTH

BATES MOLYNEAUX -SIXTH

DU QUOIN, ILLINOIS · AUG. 24, 1958

Above: These promotional posters put out by the factory claimed every grain of glory to be had! While Carroll Resweber is the prominently named rider, Joe Leonard and Brad Andres were also to become famous riders.

Below: This beautiful machine was built as a replica of Texan Carroll Resweber's KR750. The posters on the left boast of some of his successes in 1958 and 1959, but he actually won national titles in 1958, 1959, 1960, and 1961.

The factory gave in to demands for competition versions of the Sportster with the introduction of the XLR—this was a stripped down machine intended for TT scrambles and dirt track racing. The engine had many special parts fitted; it had a magneto fitted above the front engine mount, and also had different pistons, heads, valves, crank, and cams. The crank spun on roller bearings—these were very strong, and together with the shorter stroke, it meant that the engine could be revved hard for extended periods.

In stripped form, the bikes weighed about 300 lb, which coupled with about 80 hp made them potent machines. The XLR engines were not only used on dirt-tracks, however—many people used them for

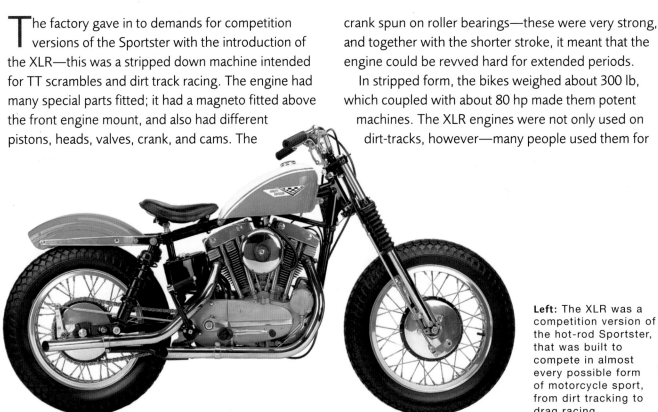

Left: The XLR was a competition version of the hot-rod Sportster, that was built to compete in almost every possible form of motorcycle sport, from dirt tracking to drag racing.

other purposes, including hillclimbing, road racing, drag racing, and for land speed record attempts. In the late 1960s a Manx Norton chassis was used to house an XLR motor. This was used to great effect in the European GP series, and raised the eyebrows of many people who thought that all Harleys were slow old machines. The factory was pleased to be able to claim a new record at

Bonneville in 1970, when a streamliner ridden by Cal Rayborn and powered by an XLR motor was recorded at an impressive 265 mph.

Right: Although the engine looked superficially similar to that fitted to the Sportster, it had many internal differences. These parts included high-performance cylinder heads, flywheels, pistons, and camshafts. It also had modifications to improve reliability, such as uprated crankshaft bearings.

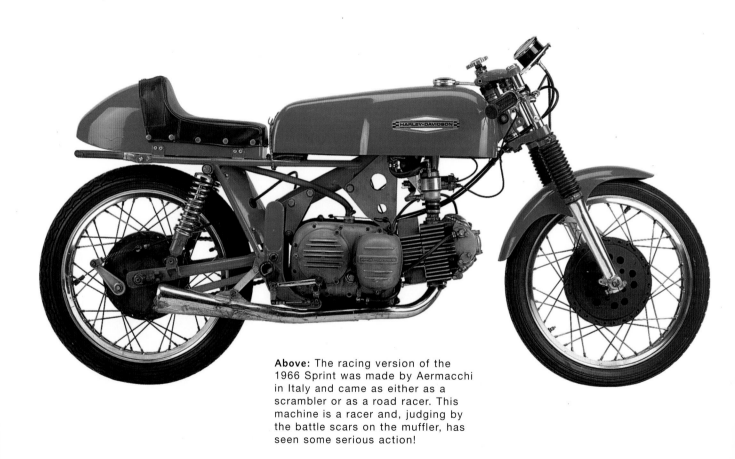

Above: The racing version of the 1966 Sprint was made by Aermacchi in Italy and came as either as a scrambler or as a road racer. This machine is a racer and, judging by the battle scars on the muffler, has seen some serious action!

HARLEY-DAVIDSON WINS!

GEORGE ROEDER

FIRST in 6 min. 53.33 sec.

7-MILE NATIONAL
SAN JOSE, CALIF. SEPT. 3, 1967

MERT LAWWILL FOURTH ON HARLEY-DAVIDSON

GEORGE ROEDER

HARLEY DAVIDSON WINS 68

HARLEY-DAVIDSON WRECKING CREW WINS SEVENTH STRAIGHT NATIONAL

6/16 — CAL RAYBORN SHATTERS LOUDON RECORD AT 73.759 MPH
TIME OF RACE: 1 hour 21 minutes 59 seconds

6/23 — WALT FULTON TAKES HEIDELBERG MINIATURE ROAD RACE
TIME OF RACE: 20 minutes 36 seconds

Above and right: These two promotional posters trumpet the race successes of the factory riders. Mert Lawwill and George Roeder went on to become famous racers; Cal Rayborn, however, became a legend.

Harley Legends: KRTT

The ill-fated K model of 1952, which only lasted for two years, had a successful racing brother called the KR. This had a 45 ci. hot rod motor that was worked on endlessly by tuning specialists throughout the United States. Incredibly, the old side-valve engine was still in production more than fifteen years later, by which time the power output had gone up from 38 to over 60 hp. It was used in many forms of competition, including for road racing in the form of the beautiful machine pictured here, which was known as the "KRTT."

The KRTT had a specially built frame, called the "Lowboy." This was constructed from steel tubing, and had a much lower steering head than previous frames. This was to help keep the frontal area to a minimum, in order to reduce wind-drag. It had a large, four leading, shoe drum front brake, high gearing, modern suspension, a massive gas tank, and streamlined bodywork. In this form the bike would do a maximum of about 140 mph. The KRTT was successful on road race tracks the world over, and is now highly sought-after for use in Vintage racing, as well as for display in museums and private collections.

Below: The 1968 KRTT shown here was hopelessly out-of-date by the time it was produced, and it was only the exceptional riding skills of Cal Rayborn that gave it wins at Daytona in 1968 and 1969.

Right: The people at the factory had realized early on in the history of the company that after sales—such as chain lubricants, and engine oils, were a vital part of the company's income.

MORE MILES from YOUR CHAINS

HALF PINT 50¢

use only

HARLEY-DAVIDSON CHAIN SAVER

SOLD EXCLUSIVELY BY HARLEY-DAVIDSON DEALERS

Printed in U.S.A.

Opposite: Probably the greatest rider to have raced a Harley-Davidson since WWII, Cal Rayborn was a past master of his craft. Tragically, he was killed in New Zealand in the early 1970s, while testing a Suzuki racer.

Above: The CRTT was extremely competitive in its native Europe, and in the world championship, but there were no national competition classes for it to compete in the United States.

Left: The RR250 was another machine built by Aermacchi and badged as a Harley-Davidson. It was a competitive bike in the right hands, but was eventually outclassed by the new Yamaha TZ250.

Right: The RR250 took two world championship titles in 1974 and 1975 with Walter Villa at the controls. Its success was partly down to the fact that it was designed as a pure racer—no road versions were ever built, and so no compromises had to be made during the design process.

The XR750 has won more races than any other motorcycle, ever. For many enthusiasts, it is also one of the most beautiful machines ever to have been built. It was born at a time when the old side-valve Harleys were being hammered by British racing bikes, and the need for a replacement was evident to all concerned. The first XR was built in 1969, and featured a de-stroked XLR engine. It had iron barrels with inadequate cooling fins, which caused it to overheat. It was slower than its predecessor, and before long the factory produced the alloy XR to replace it.

The alloy motor no longer overheated, thanks to large numbers of cooling fins. The combustion chambers worked really well, and performance was exemplary. This version of the XR750 engine was a much better proposition, and it was not long before it started scoring win after win, and for years after it ruled the dirt tracks, beating everything the British and Japanese could throw at it. They are still used to this day, albeit in updated form.

The styling of the XR750 is timeless, with twin exhausts on the left side, and two massive air cleaners on the right—all this matched up to sleek bodywork and clean lines, uncluttered by unnecessary components. The XR has spawned many aftermarket companies to produce look-alike components to transform the otherwise unexciting Sportster into the bike that Harley-Davidson should have marketed, but didn't.

SPECIFICATIONS

Engine	Ohv 45deg V-twin
Displacement	45 ci. 750 cc
Transmission	4 speed
Horsepower	90 bhp
Wheelbase	57 in
Weight	320 lb
Top Speed	130 mph

Right: To a racer, the XR750 is one of the most beautiful motorcycles ever made. This was so when it was first made in 1970, and it was still true when this 1992 machine was built.

Below: In the 1980s the factory was still competing in dirt track events—and still winning. This poster proclaims the success achieved by Scott Parker at the Indy Mile in August 1985.

Above: Since the Harley-Davidson factory no longer manufactures small capacity machines, it uses Rotax engines to compete in the smaller classes.

Opposite: Ranked alongside Carroll Resweber and Jay Springsteen, Scott Parker was one of the most natural riders on two wheels. Here he shows his winning style—he is taking this turn at over 100 mph, and yet he manages to make it all look almost effortless.

HARLEY-DAVIDSON Wins Indy Mile, Sets New Record

Harley-Davidson factory rider Scott Parker won his first ever Indianapolis, Indiana Mile Race on August 25, 1985 in a big way. Not only did he take the checkered flag, but he broke the race time record by 7.288 seconds.

Credit for this tremendous victory goes to Scotty's hard charging riding ability, a perfect track and an all night session putting the bike together by tuner Bill Werner.

Harley Legends: Spirit of Semtex

This is my own bike, which I built myself—with some considerable help from a good friend. Designed for sprint-hillclimb racing, it is an uncompromising machine, returning between three and five mpg. It is constructed from special lightweight materials, including titanium, magnesium, and carbon fiber, which were used extensively for fasteners, wheels, exhausts, and many other ancillary components. Most of the rest of it is made from aircraft Duralumin. Consequently, it doesn't weigh very much—depending on which race-parts are fitted, it scales about 330 lb.

Although the engine started out as an Evolution 1340, there are few original parts left. It now has four valve heads, a short-stroke crank, heavy duty crankcases,

Left: This machine was built for sprint-hillclimb racing, where the paved uphill tracks are anything up to a mile long, with many turns, varying from tight to ultra fast.

SPECIFICATIONS

Engine:	OHV 8-valve 45deg V-twin
Displacement:	1232 cc
Bore & stroke:	90mm x 97mm
Carburation:	2 x twin throat Weber IDF
Transmission:	4 speed wide ratio
Horsepower:	130 bhp
Wheelbase:	55 in
Weight:	330 lb

race-car pistons, dual downdraught carburetors, race ignition, and so on. The transmission is a four speed wide-ratio Quaife racing unit, and is driven by a toothed belt primary through a lightweight competition clutch.

The frame is fabricated from 7020 triple-box section aircraft alloy, and contains the oil tank—it also inherently acts as an oil cooler at the same time. Most of the cycle parts are very special Grand Prix race items, including the front forks, triple trees, front and rear brakes, both wheels, rear shock absorber, and so on.

Having so little weight, and about 130 bhp (with torque to match), it is brutal to ride, and by the time it has been warmed up, the one gallon gas tank ensures the one mile tracks it was designed for are about as far as it can go.

Above: A close-up view of the left side of the bike reveals the Interspan ignition system, belt primary, racing clutch, and massive triple box-section frame spars.

Above: The rear suspension unit is from a Grand Prix racing bike, and is operated by a fully adjustable sub-frame, giving maximum adjustability.

Opposite: A member of the Redskins race team runs his Sportster through a tight turn as part of a popular one-make series that was sponsored by the Harley-Davidson factory.

Below: This machine was built to compete in the 883 Twin Sports series. Tight regulations meant that only small changes could be made to the bikes. This kept the racing close, exciting, and economical.

Above: Bartels Harley-Davidson of Marina Del Ray in California have been involved with performance and racing Harleys for many years. This machine is a Sportster-based dirt tracker. The original bike has been stripped-out and fitted with performance items such as the seat and exhaust system.

Opposite: The front exhaust of "Spirit of Semtex" is routed to give the tire as much clearance as possible.

Right: The oil tank sight glass is clearly visible on the frame spar. The frame is made from a triple box extrusion, and holds four pints of synthetic racing oil. The motor is a high rpm short-stroker with light flywheels; four valve cylinder heads are by Fueling Engineering.

Custom Bikes 9

Arlen Ness built this incredible machine as a homage to the styling of 1950s automobiles—hence the play on the word "nostalgia." He has been building custom bikes in the Bay Area of San Francisco for over thirty years, and as a result of his dedication and hard work, his incredible creations have made him the most famous customizer in the motorcycle world. Many of his machines are styling exercises that seriously push the boundaries of what has been attempted before. Pretty well all of them also test the fabrication abilities of the craftsmen who've been tasked with implementing the unusual designs.

Arlen's machines generally start out as initial sketches, from which workshop drawings are derived. These are then used by the panel beaters as a guide while they shape the metal sections by hand using a variety of hammers, shot bags, and other specialized tools. Once the shape has been created, all the pieces—usually

Left: Absolutely everything about this machine is remarkable, from the outrageously styled bodywork to the neatly routed exhaust system.

aluminum, have to be polished to remove any tooling marks. This is a long and tiresome process, calling for the greatest degrees of skill and patience.

Right: This is Arlen Ness himself proudly sitting astride Ness-Stalgia outside the showrooms of his world famous custom motorcycle business.

Below: No matter where you look—from under the bodywork to the detailing of the engine, all you see is craftsmanship of the highest order.

Right: This Sportster-engined machine is known as "Corsa," and was built by Battistinis, a company who worked closely with Arlen Ness as a distributor of the Ness range of products. It uses many such components to good effect, creating a motorcycle to be proud of.

Opposite: The louvered bodywork on Corsa was inspired by a similar arrangement used on the sides of the Ferrari Testarossa. The high level exhaust pipes are wisely snaked in behind the cylinders to avoid burning the rider's legs.

Above: This incredible machine was built to deliver, and with the assistance of nitrous oxide injection, it does. The complex array of fuel hoses and gas bottle lines are necessary if the engine is going to receive all its vital fluids in sufficient quantities.

Right and far right: Half drag bike, half chopper, it is certainly unique, and could only be ridden by someone tall enough to reach the handlebars and the pegs at the same time. It was built by Big Al, and he is just such a man.

Opposite: This sleek machine is another example to have emerged from the workshops of Arlen Ness. Like so many of his other creations, it blends the trademark Ness billet aluminum components, such as the air cleaner housing and engine covers, with beautifully crafted sheet metalwork.

Right: Attention to detail is vital when designing a high-end custom bike. On the front wheel, even the full-floating brake rotors are emblazoned with the Arlen Ness logo. The brake calipers themselves are six piston units normally reserved for high-performance racing bikes.

Opposite: This fine machine is another example to have been built by Battistinis. It combines traditional styling with modern performance and construction techniques, making full use of the presence of high handlebars and flamed paint to stake its claim.

Above: The look of this bike is tastefully completed by the use of Ness-Tech/Bub Upsweep exhaust pipes and mufflers, which match in with the lines of the machine very well. The deep rear fender is offset by the minimalist item fitted to the front end.

Left: The engine bristles with Ness's own billet components, including the meticulously installed primary case, coil mount, forward controls, and footboards. Many other parts have been mirror polished or chrome plated, to give a stunning effect overall.

Opposite: This Shovelhead-engined Arlen Ness machine uses a rigid frame, fatbob gas tanks, high handlebars, and a flamed paintjob to create a traditionally styled machine with many up-to-date features.

This belt-driven Arlen Ness creation showcases many things. For a start, it shows off characteristic Ness styling, with swept bodywork, a two-element rear swinging arm, and pull-back handlebars. It also has superbly applied graphical paintwork, without the slightest trace of a blemish or fault—the sign of a master craftsman at work! The chrome plating is also top class, as is the beautifully executed polishing.

The closest attention to detail is evident from the tip of the front tire to the end of the rear fender. For instance, the ignition coils are hidden behind the left-hand side panel, while the plug leads are carefully routed and held in place with small clamps. Close inspection will reveal that every part has been installed with similar great care and consideration.

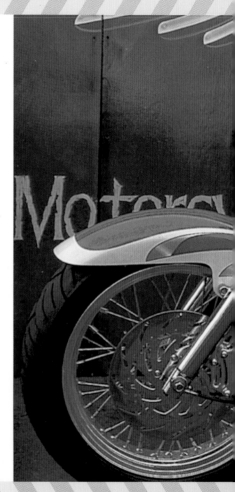

Right: This Arlen Ness machine is the epitome of a well thought out custom bike, blending as it does subtle style, superb detailing, and excellent construction techniques.

Opposite: An Arlen Ness creation takes a lot of hard work —patience, dedication, and a great deal of talent are absolute pre-requisites. Either that, or a large supply of cash would be needed to pay someone else to do it all....

Above: This Arlen Ness machine has an engine comprising a set of Shovelhead alternator crankcases onto which a Knucklehead top end has been grafted. The overall theme is that of a drag bike, with competition-style lightening holes visible on various prominent components.

Opposite: This beautiful sleek machine was built by the crew at Battistinis—hence the name "Batt Boyz," incorporated in the paintwork on the gas tank. It was built using many Arlen Ness components, including lots of billet parts on the engine.

Right: The quality of the paintwork on a custom machine is one of the first things it will be judged by, and so the top custom builders go to extraordinary lengths to get both the scheme and the standard of workmanship right.

Above: This rubber mount Softail custom was built by Graham Duffy as a showcase for his business making high-quality custom bike components. The outstanding workmanship is evident throughout the bike.

Left: The machine is based around a 1997 Evolution motor which has been taken out to 93 ci., and features Delkron cases, an S&S crank, rods, and pistons, an Andrews cam, and many other high performance parts.

Opposite: Graham machined up all manner of parts on this bike, including both wheels—the rear has a highly unusual inboard mounted disc. He also made the triple trees, forward controls, muffler caps, and much else besides.

Above: The Ness Daytec Softail chassis ensures a smooth ride. Power is delivered to the rear wheel via a toothed belt from a 5-speed CCI transmission; this in turn is driven by a chain primary.

Right: The front end comprises a set of 41mm "Massive Glide" triple trees and lower legs, onto which Performance Machine "Flamed" brake calipers and discs are attached.

Opposite: This lovely machine—known as Stinger—was built by Battistinis around a 1997 114 ci. S&S motor. This was a powerplant that justified the bike's name! It used Ness billet covers and exhaust.

Harley Legends: **Arlen Bike**

This incredible machine is yet another creation to have been born out of Arlen Ness's fertile imagination. It demonstrates how style and craftsmanship can be combined to construct a highly unusual and thought provoking piece of functional art. While never intended for long distance work, it is still practical enough to be used for cruising boulevards and runs to local bars!

The flowing lines of the hand beaten aluminum bodywork on this bike hark back to the glory days of 1930s' luxury cars, when style was considered to be everything that mattered. Successfully incorporating such features into the design of a motorcycle is far from trivial—the panel work alone must have been a labor of love. No doubt the assembly order was very carefully thought out, but even so, fitting the bodywork without scratching the paint must have been a nightmare.

Left: With its flowing lines, this exotic machine was inspired by the elegance of the cars driven by movie stars and business moguls in the 1930s.

Opposite: The hand-beaten aluminum bodywork is a masterpiece of craftsmanship and ingenuity. Combined with the superb engine detailing, this bike really stands out from the crowd.

Left: Coupe De Ville is another fine example of the superb machines built by Battistinis. It is based around a 1994 80 ci. Evolution motor with Edelbrock cylinders and heads, Ness billet covers, and a Ness Supertrapp exhaust.

Opposite: The frame dates from 1997, but has been stretched by five inches and has 35 degrees of rake. Ness Wide Glide triple trees hold the forks in place, and the bike rolls on Performance Machine Aero wheels.

Opposite: The brief received by Battistinis was to take a stock Dyna Glide and turn it into a custom machine that was also a practical road bike, without making any major alterations to either the engine or chassis.

Right: The fact that this machine was the subject of superb attention to detail can be seen from every perspective—from the simple but effective paintjob, to the meticulously executed plating and polishing on the front wheel.

Below: These are the parts that came off! The triple trees, front forks, swing arm, shocks, wheels, and brakes were all replaced with a tasteful mixture of Ness and Performance Machine billet components. Many other bolt-on parts were also changed for more stylish items.

Left and opposite: These two Fat Boys were built by Battistinis to demonstrate that stunning customs could be constructed using only parts sourced from the Ness and Performance Machine catalogs. That they succeeded is self-evident—both bikes were brand new when the project was started, but finished as you see them.

Although the two bikes started out identical, there are many subtle differences between them now, such as the air cleaner housings, the exhaust systems, the front fenders, the headlights, and so on. The major difference is, of course, the paintwork!

Left: The use of flames as a theme for custom paintjobs goes back several decades, especially with fifties hot rods, but the tasteful manner in which these have been applied make this machine stand out from the crowd even today.

Opposite: There are high handlebars, and there are *very* high handlebars! This effect is accentuated by the short springer front end, which together with the upswept fishtail pipes and short sissy bar make this a very distinctive and stylish custom.

Harley Legends: Arlen Bike

This amazing-looking custom bike is yet another machine to have been born out of Arlen Ness's unparalleled design skills. Its central styling cue is the shape of a teardrop, and this concept has been used to good effect in creating the most unusual fenders to have been seen on a motorcycle in a long time.

The continuity of design is carried through from the shape of the fenders to the lines of the gas tank, the handlebars, and especially to the curvaceous exhaust system. The geometry of the engine is also reflected in the shape of the air cleaner housing. The lower parts of the fenders can be unbolted and removed in order for the wheels to be changed in the event of a puncture, or as part of routine maintenance.

Overall, the machine itself is very clean, with very few components interrupting the smooth flowing look of the distinctive bodywork. Careful thought is needed when riding this machine, since holes in the road and kerbstones present a real threat to the well being of the lower parts of this bike's anatomy!

Right: The dramatic and unusual look of the bodywork on this classic Arlen Ness creation makes it easily recognizable, even from a distance.

Opposite: The low, solid nature of this lowrider contrasts well with the long and sleek form of many other custom bikes. With its chunky tires, massive suspension, and capacious gas tank, this machine represents a practical long distance custom.

Right: The Evolution engine in this bike is very well detailed, with an oil pressure gauge, an oil cooler, and braided oil lines. Such features will add to the reliability of any motorcycle, by helping keep the engine temperatures down.

Right: This Softail Rubbermount was built by Battistinis as a rolling test bed for their product development program. It is the ultimate in muscle-engined custom bikes, with the motor using four-cam billet crankcases by Delkron, and displacing a massive 125 ci.

Left: This Battistinis-built FXST uses an 89 ci. Evolution motor with Carl's Speed Shop heads and cam, mounted in a modified Softail frame. Onto this, Battistinis' own gas tank has been matched with Ness fenders to create a fine-looking custom.

Opposite: The Softail frame is used extensively by custom builders since it gives effective rear suspension, while still displaying the clean lines of a traditional rigid chopper. With modified Evolution engines capable of putting out serious horsepower, this helps to keep both rider and machine in one piece.

Opposite: This machine was built by Battistinis based on the design ethos of the Dyna Low Rider. It uses an 80 ci. Evolution engine, onto which Patrick Racing billet cylinder heads have been grafted, along with an S&S carb.

Above: The frame has been stretched by five inches, and raked out to 40 degrees—this gives it a long, low, look, which is accentuated by the use of Performance Machine "Twister" wheels and matching brake disc rotors.

When Arlen Ness revealed this machine—named "Smoothness"—the motorcycle world rocked on its heels. Being built around a rubber-mounted 80 ci. Evolution motor, it would be smooth to ride, but the name becomes much more apt when the incredible bodywork is considered. Fabricated by hand from sheet aluminum by Craig Naff, it must have taken blood sweat and tears to get it to this standard of finish.

The engine was rebuilt using many S&S parts, and billet covers were used all over the motor, primary case, and transmission; matching billet handlebar controls continue the theme. The sweeping slash cut exhaust pipes were specially manufactured in house to blend in with the flowing lines of the bodywork, which also boasts some beautifully constructed grilles over the headlamp, and air intakes for the engine and front brakes. As is usual with Arlen's creations, the final assembly of this masterpiece was absolutely meticulous.

Left: With its highly unusual bulbous bodywork, this has to be one of the most distinctive custom motorcycles ever built.

Opposite: Arlen Ness's creations are considered by many to be works of art, and indeed, have often been exhibited in art galleries.

Left: This incredible machine shows that it need not take years to build a distinctive custom—built by Battistinis, this FXR called "Warbird" only took four weeks to construct. In order to minimize the build-time, the frame was only given cosmetic touches, before being painted.

Opposite: The engine was given considerable attention, receiving S&S cases, Edelbrock Performer cylinder heads, and a Crane Fireball cam. The S&S Super E carburetor nestles behind a Ness Airscoop air-cleaner, and the exhaust gases exit through a Supertrapp muffler.

Above: This machine was named "Bike X." Here the finishing touches are being applied in the workshop before its maiden voyage.

Opposite: Resplendent in its yellow and white paintwork, the customer must have been happy to take this bike home.

Right: The owner of this incredible machine refused to give up riding when he lost a leg, and so moved over to three wheels to stay "on the road." It uses a Jaguar independent rear axle, which gives good functionality as well as looking suitably strong.

Opposite: The engine uses RevTech cylinder heads and a Carls' Speed Shop Typhoon carburetor, along with many billet parts including pushrod tubes, lifter blocks and outer covers. The exhaust pipes follow a tortuous route past the transmission and exit between the rear wheels.

Left: The engine was built using a Crane cam and ignition, an S&S carburetor and Ness billet rocker covers, air cleaner housing, lifter blocks, pushrod tubes, primary case, oil pressure gauge mount, and timing case.

Opposite: This machine—known as "Fat Tracker"—was built around a more or less stock frame, but with the addition of a whole host of bolt-on parts, including many billet parts such as the Laser-style Performance machine wheels, front end, fender struts, and forward controls.

Harley Legends: Arlen Smooftale

When Arlen Ness constructed the frame for "Smoothness," he made an extra one at the same time. Believe it or not, Battistinis used the "spare" one to build this bike, known as "Smooftale." It is hard to see how two such radically different bikes could be so similar under the skin. It took Jeff Duval eight months to complete the project, using an in-house aluminum gas tank mounted on the Ness frame, which nestles up next to the minimalist seat, which was machined up by Dave Batchelor. The beautiful machine Jeff Duval built was finished in Cadillac Candy Red—this was skillfully applied by Jeff McCann, having first received meticulous molding by Terry Spencer. The stunning lines of the bike are complemented by the upswept exhaust system, which was made in-house by Battistinis' own craftsmen.

Left: The left side of the bike reveals a Ness billet primary case, coil cover, and side stand mount.

The bike was completed using a wide variety of Ness billet items, including handlebar controls, cylinder head rocker covers, timing case, and air cleaner housing. The clean look is helped by the wire-spoked wheels, single front disc brake, small headlight, tiny front fender, and small diameter front forks.

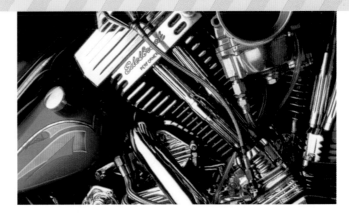

Above right: The engine was built using Edelbrock Performer cylinder heads, with Ness billet lifter blocks, pushrod tubes, and timing case.

Right: The right side of the bike shows how the lines of the bike are complemented by the specially made exhaust system.

Opposite: This machine, dubbed "FXRSS," is another creation to have come out of the Battistinis' workshops. It was built jointly by Jeff Duval and Steve Cox as a design exercise around what started out as a stock FXR.

Right: The frame has five inches of stretch and 40 degrees of rake, giving it a "kicked out" look that is appropriate to the overall styling of the bike. It has an 88 ci. hot-rod motor that was built by Carl's Speed Shop in Santa Fe Springs.

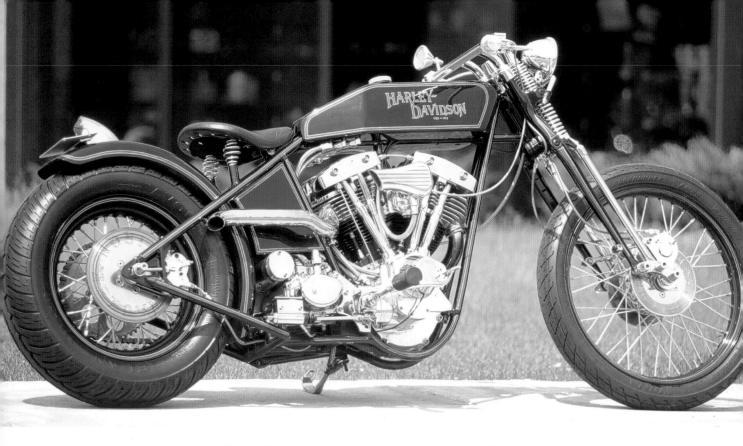

Above: This gorgeous machine uses a Shovelhead motor mounted in a rigid frame, with the overall styling modeled on the look of early 1920s bikes. The short pipes are redolent of those on a board track racer, and the springer front end finishes the period feel off beautifully.

Above: Although the bike is styled to look old, it cleverly uses modern disc brakes. Note the "Milwaukee Iron" lettering on the wheel hub.

Right: One look at this machine is enough to know that it was assembled by a very experienced builder. The attention to detail and sheer engineering quality shine through as evidence of years of wrenching on Harleys.

Above: There is some highly unusual engineering to be seen on this machine—take a look at the swing arm, and floating rear caliper mount, for instance. These parts have been beautifully machined out of solid aluminum billet.

Left: Every possible detail on this bike has been carefully thought through. Even the cables and hoses have their own individually machined billet clamps to ensure that they sit exactly where the builder intended.

Above: It's hard to know where to look on a machine like this! At first, the wild colors and lurid graphics draw one's attention away from the engineering, but when that moment has passed, the superbly finished components—such as the lovely billet wheels—make their presence felt.

Above: The outer covers of this supercharged Sportster engine have received many hours of patient attention from an experienced engraving artist. Several of the parts which were not engraved were gold plated instead, including the twin throat, side-draught carburetor.

Left: If Arlen Ness was to put all the bikes he's built together, he'd need a building the size of an aircraft hangar! Here, three of his machines can be seen basking in the glory of delighted onlookers.

Above: There are many different paint styles used on custom bikes, including multi-colored graphics with no lettering, such as that on the gas tank of this trike.

Right: The legendary manufacturer's name can be presented in many ways, as shown here on this radical supercharged Shovelhead.

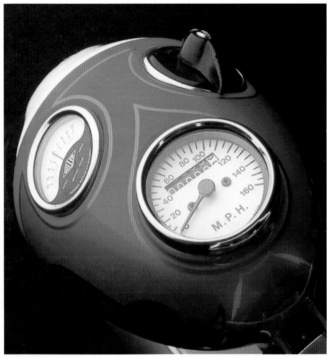

Above and left: Instruments can be mounted in many different ways. Many old bikes had the speedometer fitted into the headlight shell, but since the 1950s it has been common practice for Harley-Davidsons to use a central dash in which to site the clocks and switches.

Above: Although this machine looks like one, it is in fact a "Big Dog," which uses no Harley-Davidson parts at all. This particular example was built in a retro mode with fishtail exhausts, deep fenders, and many other period style components.

Right: Here is another look-alike machine built by Big Dog—this one was constructed in a contemporary style using high handlebars, fat bob gas tanks with central dash, a bobbed rear fender, and many other parts that would be instantly recognizable to any Harley fan.

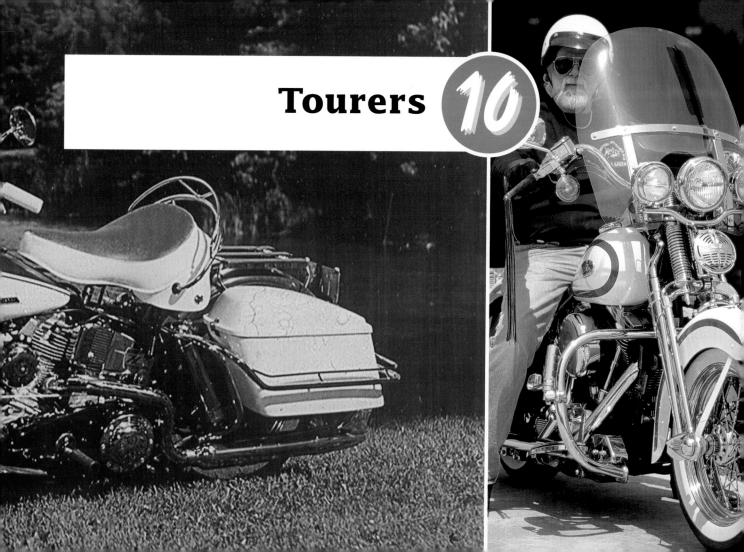

Tourers 10

Left: Harley-Davidson is probably unique in the automotive and motorcycling industries in terms of just how many of the employees ride or drive the company's product. The depth of passion and loyalty expressed within the walls of the factory have made it what it is today—a great success.

Opposite: These two machines are as American as they get—a Kenilworth truck, and a Harley-Davidson Heritage Softail dresser. Both have received loving attention from their owners in the form of extra chromed parts, improved paintwork, and hours of meticulous polishing!

Below: When the 1952 FL was released, it came with a new method of shifting gears—by a hand-operated clutch and a foot-operated lever. This caused quite a stir at the time, but it was not long before most customers realized it was significantly better than the old foot clutch/hand gearshift system.

Left: These old timers are participating in an egg and spoon race—not an activity that would normally be associated with Harley riders!

Left: This beautiful emblem of a bar and shield combined with a "V" medallion was fitted to the front fenders of 1955 models.

Below: By the time this 1955 FLH reached the public, Indian—the only other American motorcycle manufacturer—had closed down. Harley-Davidson was therefore the only domestic company left to withstand the tide of cheap European imports.

Below: The list of optional extras available to the prospective purchaser of a new Harley-Davidson was staggering; these parts included a Deluxe Buddy Seat, a Solo Seat, Dual exhausts, saddlebags, turn signals, luggage racks, fender bars, and windshields in clear, red, or blue tints!

Above: By the mid-1960s, the factory was fighting for its very survival, but the marketing department kept on putting out promotional material.

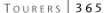

Right: This 1965 FLH Electra-Glide has the optional white trimmed Super Deluxe Buddy Seat, but it was also available in black and white, or red and white. Likewise, the fiberglass saddlebags were also available in black or white, and the tires could be stock or whitewall.

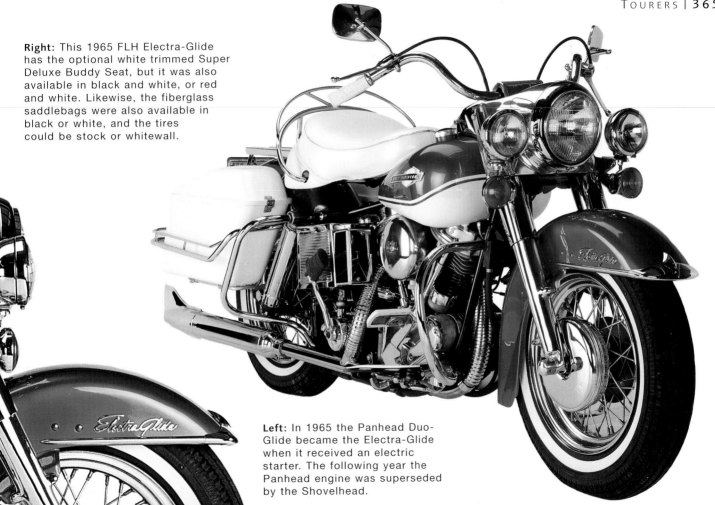

Left: In 1965 the Panhead Duo-Glide became the Electra-Glide when it received an electric starter. The following year the Panhead engine was superseded by the Shovelhead.

Harley Legends: FLH

When the Panhead engine was first introduced into the model range in 1948, it powered a range of middleweight machines, with brisk performance, and good reliability. By 1966, however, the various bikes fitted with the Panhead engine had developed into heavyweights that struggled to deliver anything more than a mediocre performance. The factory had realized this for some time, and had therefore been working on a replacement top end for the ageing Pan.

When the new motor was released in the 1966 FLH, it was given the nickname "Shovelhead," due to the somewhat spurious resemblance of the rocker boxes to coal shovels. While the new motor made more power—in the region of 60 hp—the bikes were also given electric starters, a bigger battery, and various other modifications. This increased the weight even more, by around 100 lb, to a grand total of about 780 lb; unsurprisingly, this reduced the FLH's performance to less than that of the under-powered Panhead it was meant to supersede.

At this stage, the early Shovelhead engines still used the old generator cases from the Panhead, along with the ignition unit mounted on the top of the timing case, but had new cylinder heads, rocker boxes, and ancillary parts. The extra power came from improved breathing and combustion efficiency—the heads were based on those from the Sportster, and used the same combustion chambers and valve angles.

Due to the fitment of an electric start, the model was called the "Electra-Glide"—it is unlikely that the factory realized at the time how famous this name was to become, but thanks in part to starring roles in several movies, it became an icon of sixties culture.

Left: The centrally mounted dash featuring the speedometer and switches has become an important style feature for many models in the Harley-Davidson range.

SPECIFICATIONS

Engine:	OHV 45deg V-twin
Displacement:	74 ci.
Transmission:	4 speed
Horsepower:	54 bhp
Wheelbase:	60 in
Weight:	783 lb
Top speed:	100 mph
Original price:	$1,610

Below: In 1966, the Shovelhead was introduced to the public for the first time. The FLH was a high power version of the stock FL engine.

Left: This incredible traveling light show was built in Ohio in the 1970s . While it may not be to everyone's taste, at least the owner seems to like it!

Below: This 1972 FLH shows how well parts from different decades can be used to build a machine that seems totally natural. It has panniers from the 1950s, whereas the paintwork and tank badges are straight out of the 1960s.

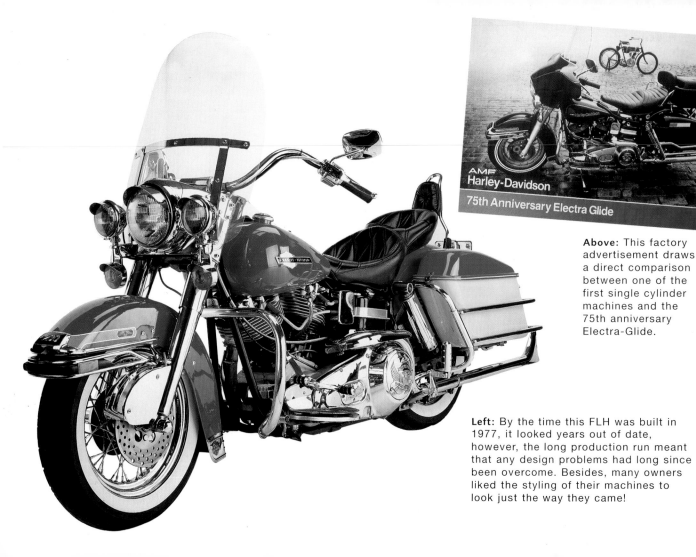

Above: This factory advertisement draws a direct comparison between one of the first single cylinder machines and the 75th anniversary Electra-Glide.

Left: By the time this FLH was built in 1977, it looked years out of date, however, the long production run meant that any design problems had long since been overcome. Besides, many owners liked the styling of their machines to look just the way they came!

Left: This Evolution-engined dresser is unmistakeable with its distinctive paintwork and the fringed leather accessories which adorn the handlebar grips and footboards.

Opposite, near right: There are a lot of names on this police model gas tank!

Opposite, far right: The red and white paintwork theme is continued from the fenders and gas tank over the hard luggage. Instead of having a top box fitted, there is a chromed carriage rack on this bike.

Above: Some Harleys have hardly any instrumentation at all, whilst others have enough to keep an airline pilot happy. There is, however, a case to be made for having such an array of gauges on a long-distance tourer. If you're on a serious run and about to enter a remote area, it's good to know that your battery is charging correctly and that the oil pressure is looking healthy.

Right: This display of lights and chrome should be enough to dissuade most tailgaters from getting too close.

Opposite: The "Ultra" designation signifies the full-dresser version of the Electra-Glide. Some models had a built-in CB radio, a stereo, cruise control, and even an intercom.

Left: This machine only has a small windshield fitted rather than a full fairing, but even this would be a big help in reducing rider fatigue over long distances. When the weather is bad, or there are a lot of bugs in the air, such a device becomes absolutely indispensable.

Opposite, near right: One of the biggest problems with using a motorcycle to transport anything is that there's often nowhere to carry it. A luggage rack such as this sturdy unit can be extremely useful—it's amazing just how much luggage can be strapped on by a determined rider.

Opposite, far right: When you're traveling long distances, you can never be sure that you're going to arrive in daylight. Covering unfamiliar roads at night becomes a lot easier with the addition of extra driving lights.

Above: Not all tourers are based around the Electra-Glide —this is a Springer dressed up for long runs.

Left: The ultra reliable Evolution engine can make good use of the large gas tanks used on this machine.

Opposite: The owner of this bike has added his own slant to its styling, with the use of aftermarket fringed saddlebags, and a solo seat.

The Electra-Glide Ultra Classic was one of the six 90th Anniversary limited edition machines produced by the Harley-Davidson factory, of which 1,340 examples were made. It was fitted with an automotive-style cruise control to make long distance riding even easier; this even had a feature which allowed adjustment of the cruising speeds. Along with the many other extras fitted as standard was a CB radio, which all together brought the showroom price up to a heady $16,099.

In an attempt to keep the center of gravity as low as possible, the

Left: With a small passenger on the pillion seat, the Ultra Classic Electra-Glide weighs half a ton.

SPECIFICATIONS	
Engine:	OHV 45deg V-twin
Displacement:	80 ci.
Transmission:	5-speed
Horsepower:	70 bhp
Wheelbase:	63 in
Weight:	780 lb
Top speed:	110 mph
Original price:	$15,349

Above: With its electronic fuel injection-equipped Evolution engine, belt final drive, and soft suspension, the Ultra Classic Electra-Glide gives a smooth ride.

Above: The Ultra Classic Electra-Glide is all about traveling in comfort, as this luxurious dual seat shows.

Above: The hard luggage fitted to the Electra-Glide range gives enough storage space to provide for a good weekend's camping.

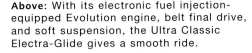

crankcase sump was extended so that less oil was carried high on the bike. This was a radical departure from the factory's previous practice, but it also had the benefit that oil temperatures could be kept down, since the exterior parts of the casting were open to the free flow of air from behind the front wheel. The ability to check the oil level was also simplified by the fitment of a dipstick. The relocation of the battery lower in the frame of the Electra-Glide Ultra Classic also helped make the machine more manageable for smaller riders by making it feel less top-heavy.

Far left: The enormous fairing provides maximum protection for the rider under almost any conditions this side of a tornado.

Left: It's usually a problem arriving at a destination on a motorcycle—where do you put your helmet if you don't want to spend the day carrying it around? Well, the top box on the Ultra Classic Electra-Glide solves this—there's enough room for both the rider and his passenger to be left with free hands.

Opposite: Full dressers— you either love them or you hate them. There's little middle ground.

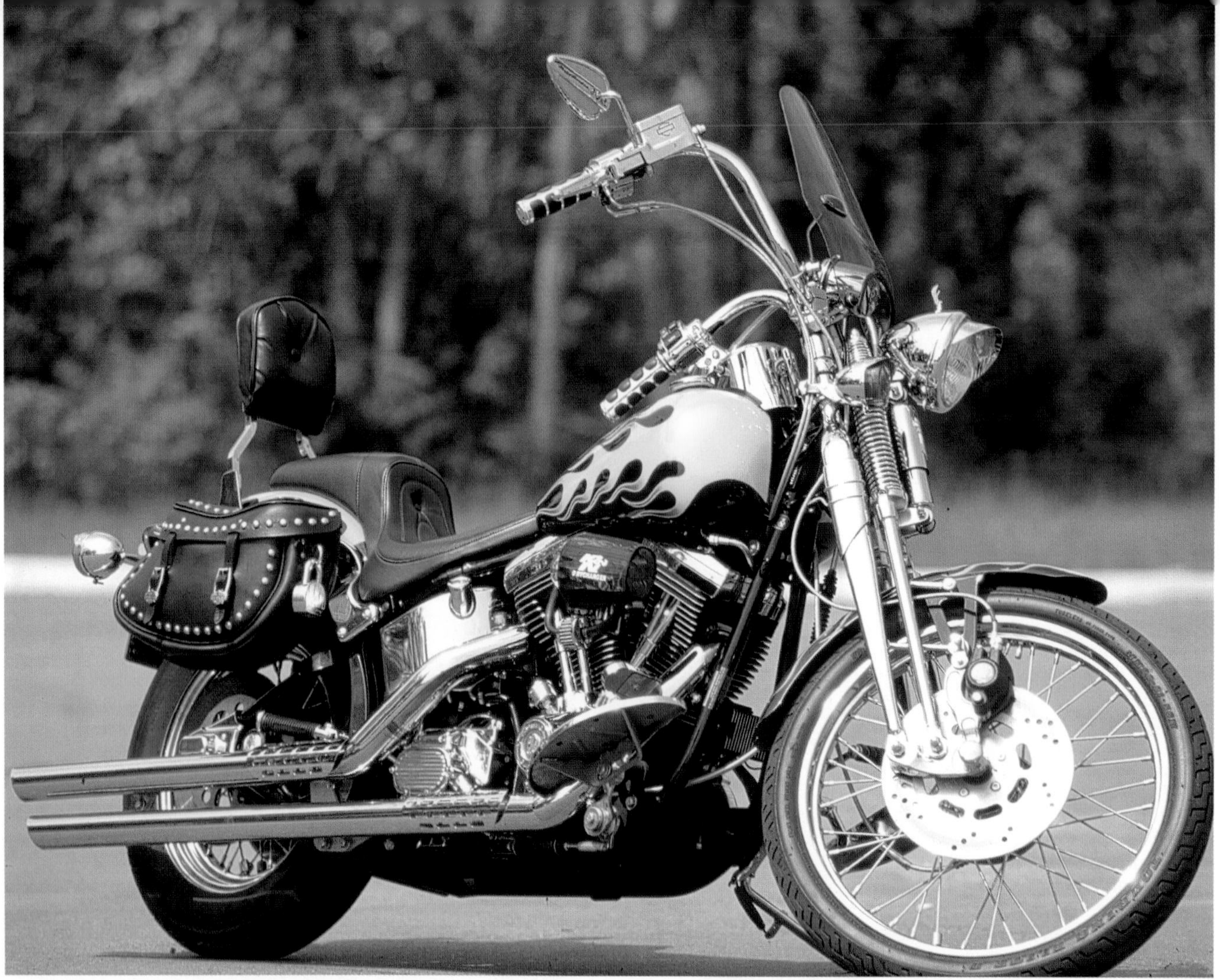

Above right: The Springer Softail uses a centrally mounted dash to mount the instruments and switchgear. This feature ties in well with the overall styling of a model that sold so well that the first year's production run had to be more than quadrupled the following year.

Above left: Soft luggage such as these traditional-style leather saddlebags can be a good choice—not only is it practical to remove and carry them around if necessary, but they look good whilst installed, giving the bike a more genuine retro look.

Right: The Springer Softail—designated the FXSTS, was first introduced to the public in 1988. At the time some questioned the wisdom of using such an old design of front end on a modern motorcycle, but the model proved so popular that several variations on the theme have since been produced.

Opposite: Flames are more usually associated with hot rods or choppers than tourers, but each to their own!

Left: The Tour Glide was first introduced to the model range in 1989, at the same time as the Electra-Glide Ultra Classic. The main difference between the models was that the Electra-Glide used a handlebar-mounted fairing, whereas the Tour Glide used the more substantial frame-mounted unit.

Opposite: One of the biggest advantages of long distance touring is that you get the chance to go and see places you've never been to before. This rider is taking the opportunity to check out the view whilst taking a brief break from his riding.

Opposite: One of the real advantages of modern electrical systems is that they have evolved to the point where they can power a whole bank of extra driving lights. This makes riding in the dark a whole lot safer and more enjoyable.

Right: In the bad old days of the unreliable Shovelhead-engined AMF era machines, sales of touring machines took a serious beating from the excellent alternatives offered from Japan. A return to private ownership for the Harley-Davidson company, and the introduction of the Evolution engine changed all this, and sales of Milwaukee's finest are once again very healthy.

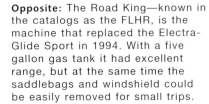

Opposite: The Road King—known in the catalogs as the FLHR, is the machine that replaced the Electra-Glide Sport in 1994. With a five gallon gas tank it had excellent range, but at the same time the saddlebags and windshield could be easily removed for small trips.

Above right: Native American Indian symbols and images are very popular sources for inspiration when it comes to one-off paintwork on motorcycles—be they custom bikes or long-distance tourers.

Above left: One of the great advantages of redesigning the paintwork on your own motorcycle is that you get the chance to add all sorts of small graphical images, some of which may mean more to you and your friends than the casual onlooker.

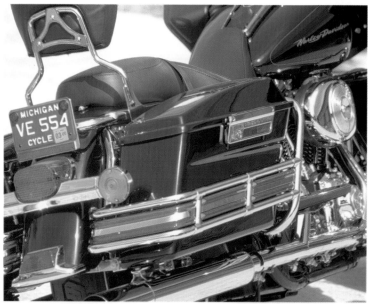

Above and left: This machine continues a long tradition of Harleys being used by police departments as regular patrol vehicles. The excellent storage space afforded by the hard luggage panniers helps an officer to carry the various types of equipment he may need. This could include emergency first aid kits, road block "stingers," wet weather clothing, and paperwork. Another vital factor as far as law enforcement agencies are concerned is that the reliable electrical systems installed on modern Harley-Davidsons allow the radio, siren, and warning lights to function efficiently at all times.

Above: This police special uses a Twin-Cam Evolution motor to propel its master on his duties enforcing the local statutes. The bike is essentially a Road Glide tourer, but with the additional modifications required to make it suitable for use by police officers.

Above: It would seem that the saying "It's not the arriving, but the road getting there that matters" is true! This rider would probably agree, as he is clearly enjoying the magnificent view provided by the local geography.

Opposite: There's no mistaking who built this machine! It is Arlen's take on how he thinks a dresser could look. It utilizes a whole host of Ness billet components, such as rocker covers, air cleaner, timing cover, gearcase covers, and so on.

Harley Legends: FLTRI

In 1998, the Evolution engine was itself superseded by a new generation motor—this was the Twin Cam 88. As suggested by the name, it displaced a massive 88 ci. (1450cc), and featured two camshafts. This gave an immediate increase in power and torque, but also reduced noise and pollution emissions. The single cam design was something that had been around since the Knucklehead engine started the lineage off back in the 1930s—but while it had its advantages, it had drawbacks, too. Foremost was the fact that the pushrod geometry had to be compromised in order to fit everything in place. This had the knock-on effect of creating extra stresses in the pushrods, which in turn generated noise—the great enemy of air-cooled engines.

The Harley-Davidson factory was in a tight spot when it came to redesigning the Evolution engine—first and foremost was the fact that their customer base wanted big air-cooled V-twins. Unfortunately, such motors are inherently noisy—not so much from the exhaust, but from mechanical noise generated by the engine's components rattling and banging around.

To make matters worse, current noise and emissions regulations are now so strict, that it's more or less a given thing that engines have to be water-cooled. The extra thickness of the cylinder block reduces the noise of the pistons slapping against the cylinder bores. The cooling fins on air-cooled motors, however, tend to amplify any noise from within. A further advantage of liquid cooling is that the combustion chamber temperatures can be maintained at a more consistent level, reducing exhaust pollution.

The factory, therefore, did brilliantly well in managing to produce an engine that by all rights should not be

SPECIFICATIONS

Engine:	OHV 450 V-twin
Displacement:	88 ci.
Transmission:	5 speed
Horsepower:	80 bhp
Wheelbase:	63.5 in
Weight:	750 lb
Top speed:	112 mph
Original price:	$15,220

Opposite: With the introduction of the FLTRI came the first of the Twin Cam 88 engines, which was a direct descendant of the Evolution.

able to pass the regulations. It did this by investing an
enormous amount of money in research and
development, and the addition of an extra camshaft
was just one of many ways in which they reduced
emissions enough to make the grade.

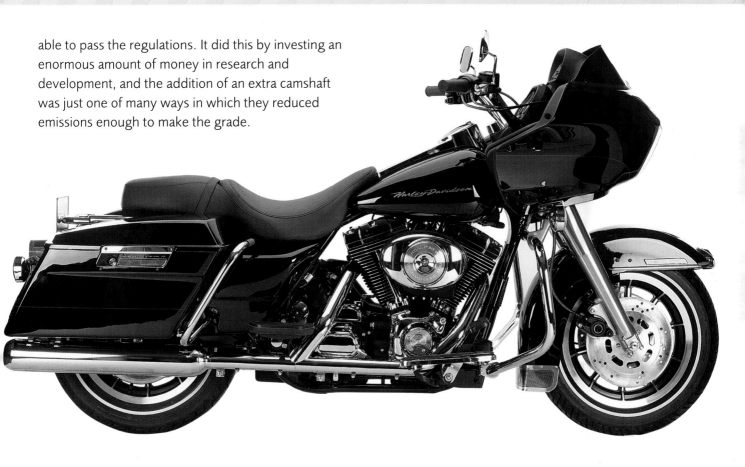

Index

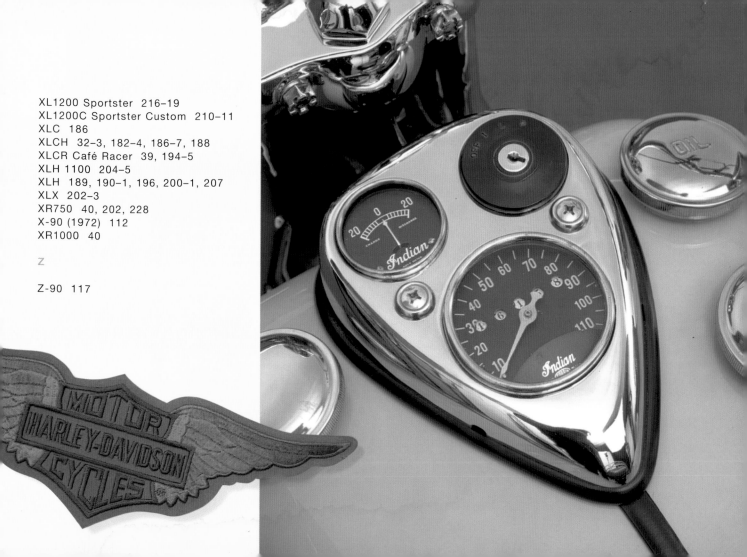

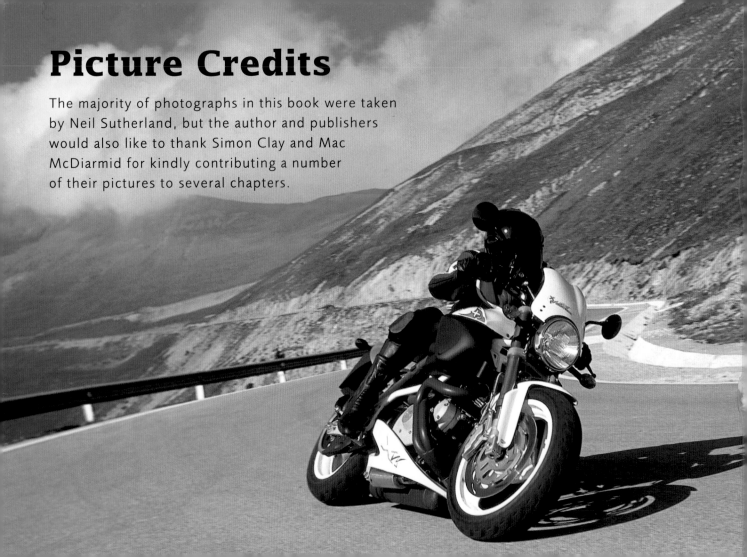

Picture Credits

The majority of photographs in this book were taken by Neil Sutherland, but the author and publishers would also like to thank Simon Clay and Mac McDiarmid for kindly contributing a number of their pictures to several chapters.